Qatar

Qatar

BY TERRI WILLIS

Enchantment of the World
Second Series

Children's Press®

A Division of Scholastic Inc.

NEW YORK   TORONTO   LONDON   AUCKLAND   SYDNEY
MEXICO CITY   NEW DELHI   HONG KONG
DANBURY, CONNECTICUT

Frontispiece: The Royal Palace, Doha

Consultant: Amy J. Johnson, Ph.D., Assistant Professor of History, Berry College, Mount Berry, GA

Please note: All statistics are as up-to-date as possible at the time of publication.

Book production by Herman Adler Design

Library of Congress Cataloging-in-Publication Data

Willis, Terri.
Qatar / by Terri Willis.
    p. cm. — (Enchantment of the world. Second series)
Includes bibliographical references and index.
 ISBN 0-516-24254-7
1. Qatar—Juvenile literature. [1. Qatar.] I. Title. II. Series.
DS247.Q3W55 2003
953.63—dc21   2003010795

Qatar

Contents

Cover photo:
Qatar National
Museum

Doha

Falcon and trainer

A Country Moving Into the Future

QATAR IS A SMALL NATION IN THE MIDDLE EAST. IT IS A part of the Arab world, and as such it shares a long cultural tradition with its neighbors. Bedouin people lived in the country's interior for centuries, creating a colorful culture amid the desert setting. They raised animals and grew date palms. Their blankets and baskets were beautifully crafted and decorated with intricate designs. Other early inhabitants of the peninsula lived on the coast, and they made a good living by harvesting pearls from the surrounding waters.

Today most Qatari citizens live in cities. Qatar is a wealthy country, thanks to the petroleum beneath its surface. The country's government is a traditional monarchy, with a ruling family whose members have held power for more than a century. The current ruler, or emir, is Shaykh Hamad bin Khalifa al-Thani, who came to power in 1995.

Nearly all its citizens are Muslim. They worship the same god that Christians and Jews do, and they refer to God as "Allah." They are required by their religion to pray daily and to donate money to the poor. They are prohibited from drinking alcohol, and most women wear long, flowing robes that cover their bodies and veils that cover their hair. The Sharia, Islam's body

Opposite: **Doha harbor is Qatar's main seaport.**

Most Qataris wear traditional clothing.

The peninsula that makes up Qatar juts into the Persian Gulf.

of laws, governs Qatar. Its regulations shape the way that Qatari people live. Most citizens of Qatar live very conservatively.

If you look at Qatar on a map, you see that its land, like its culture, has deep roots in the Arab world. Qatar borders another Arab country, Saudi Arabia. Much of Qatar pushes into the Persian Gulf, surrounded only by water. Culturally, too, Qatar is beginning to push beyond its historical traditions.

A Changing Nation

The Qatari government has, in recent years, focused on changes in policies and economy. Top priorities include greater attention to human rights, social reform, a strong economy, and a democratic form of government.

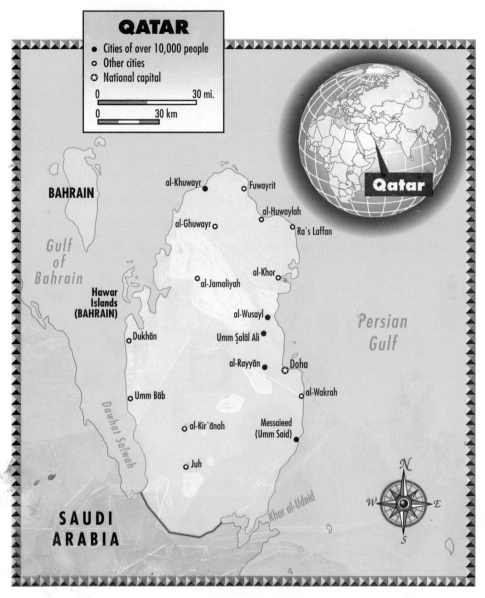

QATAR
- Cities of over 10,000 people
- Other cities
- National capital

0   30 mi.

0   30 km

BAHRAIN

al-Khuwayr   Fuwayrit

al-Huwaylah

al-Ghuwayr   Ra`s Laffan

Gulf of Bahrain

Hawar Islands (BAHRAIN)

al-Jamaliyah   al-Khor

al-Wusayl

Dukhān   Umm Ṣalāl Ali

Persian Gulf

al-Rayyān   Doha

Umm Bāb   al-Wakrah

al-Kir`ānah   Messaieed (Umm Said)

Dawhat Salwah

Juh

SAUDI ARABIA   *Khor al-Udeid*

N
W   E
S

The emir is working to give up much of his own power in an effort to convert his nation into a democracy. Qatar's first nationwide elections were held in 1999, with the aid of a small municipal council, whose members were also elected. Women were allowed to vote, and even to run as candidates, though none were elected at the time. Qatar officials are preparing a new constitution that will call for a parliamentary style of government, with citizens represented by the leaders they themselves elect.

Women are now achieving far more freedom and opportunities in Qatar than ever before. Several women hold appointed government positions, and the number of women attending the country's universities continues to grow.

Students at Virginia Commonwealth School of Arts in Doha

The U.S. military, including these U.S. soldiers at al-Sayliyah base, maintain an important presence in Qatar.

The press in Qatar has great freedom, too, even though it is not guaranteed by law. The independent news station Al-Jazeera Satellite Channel was established in 1996, the year after the emir abolished the government-run Ministry of Information. Known for breaking with tradition, Al-Jazeera criticizes some policies of regional governments. When complaints arose about this critical coverage, Qatar's emir defended Al-Jazeera. "I believe that criticism is a good thing," he said, "and some discomfort for government officials is a small price to pay for this new freedom."

The emir has himself risked criticism from neighboring nations in recent years, as he has allowed U.S. military troops to establish bases at al-Sayliyah and al-Udeid. The United States used the bases as strategic locations from which to launch its 2003 war in Iraq. Qatar and the United States have become strong allies.

The close ties between Qatar and the United States do not benefit Americans only. Qataris expect to gain from it too. They are seeking security in the Middle East, a region that has seen a great deal of conflict and war in recent years. Qataris expect the U.S. military presence to help protect them. They are also looking to the United States to help them modernize.

A new billion-dollar "Education City" has been built near the capital city of Doha. Satellite campuses from several major U.S. universities, such as Cornell University and Virginia Commonwealth University, are based here. Education City is expected to become a hub of learning for the entire region. American businesses are also moving into Doha and introducing Western culture to Qatar. A mall in the center of Doha is home to such American dining favorites as Kentucky Fried Chicken, McDonalds, and Starbucks Coffee.

American dollars are important to Qatar's future too. The country's economy is based on its vast energy reserves, and the huge investments in Qatar of U.S. oil companies help to develop the country's oil and natural gas industries. This economic strength has made Qatar one of the wealthiest countries in the world.

Despite Qatar's strong ties to the United States, its growing attention to human rights, and its push toward democracy, the nation remains firmly rooted in the Arab world. The ways in which Qatari leaders and citizens negotiate these changes will shape the country's future for decades to come.

Popular fast-food restaurants are part of the American influence in Qatar.

The Desert Land

THE GEOGRAPHY AND THE CLIMATE OF QATAR ARE ALL about contrasts. The peninsula country is mainly desert, with a hot climate. However, it is almost completely surrounded by the waters of the Persian Gulf. The desert air isn't dry, because moisture from the gulf makes it quite humid much of the year. Most of Qatar experiences a brief rainy period each year.

Opposite: **The beauty of a desert sunset**

Satellite view of the Arabian Peninsula

A Middle Eastern Nation

Qatar is a part of the Middle East, the region between Europe and eastern Asia. People living there call it *al-sharq al-awsat*, the Arabic term for "Middle East." Some people disagree about which specific countries constitute the Middle East, but those identified as Middle Eastern countries usually include Qatar, Bahrain, Egypt, Iran, Iraq, Israel, Jordan, Kuwait, Lebanon, Oman, Saudi Arabia, Syria, Turkey, United Arab Emirates, and Yemen. Other countries sometimes listed as part of the Middle East include Libya, Afghanistan, and Sudan.

About 382 million people live in the Middle East, in an area that covers about 4.6 million square miles (11.9 million square kilometers.) The largest population is in Egypt,

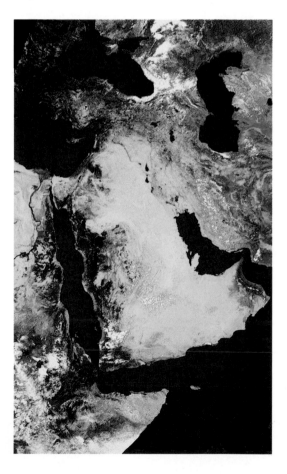

which has more than 70 million people. Sudan has the largest land area, with 917,400 square miles (2,376,000 sq km). Though Qatar is small, it is not the Middle East's smallest country. That title belongs to the tiny nearby island nation of Bahrain. Only about 5 percent of Middle Eastern land can be used to grow crops. Most of the land is desert, scrub, and mountains. But it's not wasteland; this land contains valuable

Much of Qatar contains desert, shrub, and mountain land.

Desalination

Qatar is a very dry country, so providing fresh drinking water for its citizens is always a challenge. The water of the Persian Gulf surrounds most of the nation, but it's too salty to drink. It's also too salty to use for watering crops. The water must first be desalinated. Desalination is the process that removes salt from water. It usually involves heating the water to boiling. When the water forms steam that evaporates, the salt remains behind. The steam is captured and condensed into good drinking water. Desalination is a costly process because it takes a great deal of energy to heat the water and cool the steam.

oil fields. The Middle East produces most of the world's oil, about 10 million barrels each day.

Geography of Qatar

Qatar measures 115 miles (185 km) at its longest, and is 55 miles (89 km) wide. It covers an area of 4,416 square miles (11,437 sq km). You could easily drive around its perimeter in one day, although parts of the trip would require a vehicle with four-wheel drive to get through sand dunes and places without roads. Anyone taking such a journey would see the most populated areas of Qatar, which are its cities. Most of Qatar's cities are along its coast. Very few people live in the nation's interior.

The peninsula of Qatar is flat. Most of the land is slightly above sea level. Its highest point, Qurayn Abu al-Bawl, is 338 feet (103 meters) high. The country's main physical feature is the Dukhan anticline, a shallow but broad arch running north to south throughout much of the country. It is slightly higher, above the terrain, in the west. An anticline is caused when a fold in the earth rises up to a crest and slopes downward on both sides. The small range of hills formed as a result is the

The hills of Dukhan hold petroleum below the surface.

Jebel Dukhan, or "Mountains of Dukhan." They run parallel to the west coast and contain Qatar's most important oil fields.

Limestone deposits and clays, which built up during several geological eras, form the base of the land in Qatar. The surface also has a lot of sandstone. Salt flats run along many of the country's coastal areas, but high sand dunes grace the southeast. Much of the interior is scrubby desert, covered with gravel and sand. Strong winds that blow southeasterly have eroded much of this land. These winds have also shaped the beautiful sand dunes.

Qatar controls several small islands just off the main peninsula. These islands, and the neighboring island nation of Bahrain, were all once part of a larger landmass that included the Qatar peninsula. Centuries of strong winds caused erosion and the separation of the landmasses. Among these islands are

Wind gives sand dunes their elegant shape.

Halul Island is important to the country's oil industry.

Much of Qatar's perimeter is Persian Gulf coastline

Qarradh to the west and Umm Tais and Ra's Rakan in the north. Halul, about 56 miles (90 km) off the east coast, is home to an important oil processing, storage, and export terminal. Until recently, Qatar was locked in an ownership dispute with Bahrain over the Hawar Islands to its west. In 2001, the International Court of Justice ruled that Bahrain could keep the main Hawar Island, and Qatar was granted several important maritime areas and their resources.

Qatar's Coast

Most of Qatar is surrounded by the Persian Gulf. The country's coast extends about 350 miles (563 km). Its only land border, where the country meets Saudi Arabia, is 37 miles (60 km) long. Qatar has a number of natural harbors along its coast, including Doha, Messaieed (Umm Said), and al-Wakrah. Historically these were important trading hubs, and they remain so today. The main product now shipped from these ports is petroleum.

The Inland Sea

South of Doha are miles and miles of desert. However, a long and beautiful channel of water seems to emerge from nowhere. This site, known as the Khor al-Udeid, or the Inland Sea, is on the southeast tip of Qatar, where the waters of the Persian Gulf cut into the land. This channel forms a shallow lake between Qatar and Saudi Arabia. Qatar's coast has beautiful white sandy beaches that contrast with lovely pink cliffs on Saudi Arabia's shores across the water.

Though this area is a popular tourist destination, it is not heavily developed. No resorts have been built at Khor al-Udeid. The people of Qatar wish to keep the area untouched, to maintain its beauty. Visitors can reach it by four-wheel-drive vehicle or boat, but they must camp in tents if they wish to stay there overnight. The changes in light from day to night make the view even more spectacular, as the sun casts impressive shadows across the sand dunes. It's important to be well prepared to spend the night in the desert. Fierce sandstorms and the lack of fresh drinking water can pose serious dangers. For these reasons, many Doha hotels and tourist agencies organize such outings.

The Climate

Qatar's desert climate means that the country receives limited rainfall during mild winters and hot, humid summers. Summer usually arrives in May and lasts through September. Temperatures frequently reach up to 104° Fahrenheit (40° Celsius). Although little rain falls, the air is heavy with

Qatar's Geographical Features

Area: 4,416 square miles (11,437 sq km)

Land and Water Borders: Saudi Arabia to the south and the Persian Gulf

Greatest Distance North to South: 115 miles (185 km)

Greatest Distance East to West: 55 miles (89 km)

Highest Elevation: Qurayn Abu al-Bawl, 338 feet (103 m)

Lowest Elevation: Sea level

Length of Coastline: 350 miles (563 kms)

Highest Average Temperature: 104°F (40°C) in the summer

Lowest Average Temperature: 68°F (20°C) in the winter

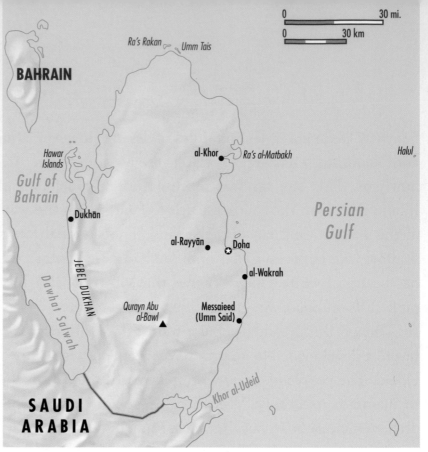

Average Annual Precipitation: Less than 2 inches (5 cm)

humidity. Ninety percent humidity is common, especially along Qatar's coast. Strong, hot winds, called *shamal*, may blow from the north across the country during the summer. They often create great dust storms and sandstorms.

Winter in Qatar usually lasts from October through April. During this time, temperatures average 68°F (20°C). The nation averages less than 2 inches (5 centimeters) of precipitation each year. Most of it falls in December, and it usually comes as drenching, severe storms. Few plants grow well in such a climate, so the terrain most often appears brown.

When the rains come, though, the land bursts into bloom. The "instant" greenery lasts only a few days.

A Look at Qatar's Cities

More than half of Qatar's population resides in the capital city of Doha, but the country has other important urban areas too. Located just west of Doha is the city of al-Rayyān, something of a suburb to Qatar's capital city. With a population of 194,800 in 2003, up from 91,996 in 1986, al-Rayyān is rapidly growing. Among its attractions is the al-Rayyān Equestrian Center, a popular place to view horse races.

A pretty city located just south of Doha is al-Wakrah, with a population of 24,400. It was once an important center for the pearl trade, but today it is a quiet fishing port. Dhows, traditional Arabic sailing boats, line its docks. The city contains several lovely white mosques and fine examples of old homes. One old home, now a museum, displays weavings and carpets made long ago by Qatar's nomadic Bedouin people.

Until recently, Messaieed was referred to as Umm Said. This city, with a population of 9,000, lies about 24 miles (39 km) south of Doha. It is mostly an industrial center with a large seaport used mainly to export hydrocarbons. It also has fine beaches. The sand dunes on Messaieed's shores are lovely, sweeping, and high. A sport that's gaining in popularity on the dunes there is sand skiing! Participants strap on skis and guide themselves down the sides of the dunes using poles, in much the same way as snow skiers do in colder climates around the world.

Dukhān, with a population of 6,400, lies near the center of Qatar's west coast, where low hills and limestone rock formations add interest to the landscape. Dukhān also has great beaches. The city is the center of the nation's oil and natural-gas industry. Qatar's national oil and gas company employs most of Dukhān's workers. Although the city has some small shops and restaurants, most residents frequently travel to Doha for major shopping excursions and to enjoy the attractions of big-city life.

On Qatar's northeast coast is the quiet fishing village of al-Khor, with a population of only 5,500 people. Times are changing in this fast-growing community. Today al-Khor is an industrial center, on its way to becoming Qatar's second-largest city because of its location near the country's important and developing North Field Gas industrial complex. Here, natural gas is taken from the ground and moved to the area's huge facilities to be compressed into liquefied natural gas (LNG). Also near the port of al-Khor is Ra's Laffan, where LNG is stored and shipped out. The city is rushing to build up its residential districts to keep up with the large number of workers coming into the area. Hospitals, schools, and other important structures are under construction as well, along with a world-class sailing resort. The city has a pretty corniche, which is a broad boulevard and walkway along the shoreline. Lined with recreational facilities, restaurants, and shops, it is a nice place to stroll.

Life in the Desert

QATAR HAS VERY LITTLE BIOLOGICAL DIVERSITY. It has few species of native plants and animals. The only animals that can survive are those that adapt to the desert climate, which features high heat, low humidity, little access to underground water, and sparse vegetation.

Opposite: **Desert flowers**

Desert Plants

Most desert plants in Qatar are low-growing shrubs, such as sage brush and the creosote bush. Each plant grows far from others to ensure that it has enough resources to survive. Some plants survive the dry conditions simply by escaping them: They turn to seed and lay dormant, sometimes for years. Then,

Desert squash has adapted to the dry environment.

Desert flowers bloom after rare rains.

when a rare, hard rain falls, they burst into bloom. Other plants remain underground as roots and bulbs to await the rains. After the rain, the desert becomes a vision of blossoming life. But it doesn't last long—these blooming plants usually survive a few days at most. Date palms grow in the low-lying areas where water collects during the winter season.

Leafy plants typically adapt to the desert by having small or waxy leaves that don't lose as much water through their pores as other plant types. Other desert plants are succulents—that is, they store water in their leaves, roots, and stems. Such roots are extensive, and they grow deep to access whatever water is available underground.

Animal life in the desert is closely tied to plant life. Plants provide food for animals, and some offer cooling shade during the day. Desert animals usually have light coloring. This reflects light and heat and keeps them from overheating. Some small mammals, reptiles, and insects stay cool by burrowing under the sand. These creatures often have special coverings, or valves, over their eyes, ears, and noses to help keep out grains of sand.

Sand gazelles' light coloring helps keep them cool.

Many birds and reptiles of the desert have an unusual way of eliminating urine. In order to keep most of the water in their bodies, they excrete only crystals of concentrated uric acid containing little to no liquid at all.

Useful Desert Plants

A number of Qatar's plants lend more than just beauty to the desert landscape. Some are also edible. Others have medicinal value—they help sick people get well. The University of Qatar is researching the country's flora to determine which plants might be useful in these ways. Among them are githgath, which can be used to treat several ailments, and jaad, a member of the mint family that helps with digestive problems. Ephedra (right) is a desert plant used to prepare ephedrine. This drug is helpful to those who suffer from nasal congestion and was once used in treating asthma. It has dangerous side effects, though, including tremors, rapid heartbeat, and mental confusion, so it's no longer commonly prescribed.

Scorpions survive by hiding from the heat during sunlight hours.

Animals of the Desert

The most common animals of Qatar are insects, such as scorpions, grasshoppers, and crickets. Scorpions thrive in tropical regions throughout the world. They're a type of arachnid, ranging from about 1 to 5 inches (2.5 to 13 cm), with narrow bodies and eight legs. Most unusual are the scorpion's two pinching claws, much like those of a small lobster, and segmented tail, which is usually curved up and forward over its back. The tail ends in a stinger that is supplied with poison from a pair of glands near the tip. Scorpions are nocturnal, hiding under rocks and other protected places during the heat of the day and moving about during the cooler night hours.

Though few scorpions are dangerous to humans, they use their claws to capture their prey of spiders and insects. The prey is killed with a poisonous sting and then crushed between

Geckos' special eyelids help them adapt to the desert.

the claws near the scorpion's mouth. The scorpion releases digestive fluid on the prey to liquefy it. Then the scorpion simply sucks it up.

Qatar's reptiles include lizards such as geckos and skinks. Geckos are small insect eaters that thrive in warm regions throughout the world. Though some are bright green, those that live in the Qatari desert are light brown and gray. Their large eyes don't have movable eyelids; instead they are covered with a thin scale that they can see through. This keeps the sand and dust out of their eyes.

Skinks are small lizards too. They spend much of their day searching for fruits and insects to eat, and they rest at night under the shelter of sand, stones, or sticks. If a skink is trapped

Skinks eat fruit and insects.

and needs to make a quick escape, it can release its tail, with no loss of blood. The tail will eventually grow back. Several types of turtles and toads also live in Qatar.

A few small mammals thrive in the Qatari desert, including jerboas, desert hares, and sand rats, which are similar to gerbils. Mammals of this type live in the dry, sandy areas throughout Africa and Asia. Sand rats can live on very little water and feed nightly on insects, grasses, and seeds. Jerboas have similar eating habits. These small rodents have short front legs and long hind legs that they use for jumping. They can jump as far as 8 feet (2.4 m) in one leap. Their long tails help to balance them when they jump.

Sand rats need little water to survive.

Qatar's National Animal

The Arabian oryx is Qatar's national animal. This endangered species is a beautiful animal. The oryx reaches a height of about 48 inches (122 cm) and can weigh as much as 450 pounds (204 kilograms). Its slender, long horns range from 20 to 50 inches (51 to 127 cm), and they have sharp points that hunters once used as spears.

The oryx feeds mainly on shrubs and grasses, and it drinks from waterholes fed by deep underground wells. If water isn't readily available, the oryx can go for weeks without it. However, it needs to replace that water by eating foods with a high water content, such as melons.

At one time, this rare type of gazelle roamed wild through the Qatari countryside, living near natural wells and oases. But as the underground wells were tapped to provide water for humans and the sources of water in the wild disappeared, the oryx population began to drop. Overhunting also reduced the oryx population, and many once believed that the oryx was extinct. Today, however, Arabian oryx still live in Qatar. They are protected and bred in special reserves established by the government.

Life in the Sea and Air

Sea life abounds in the water surrounding Qatar. Some of the marine animals in this area are quite dangerous to humans; among them are dragonfish and stonefish, sea snakes, and jellyfish. The stonefish is one of the most venomous verte- brates known. It has a large head and spiny fins that contain poison. Since it inhabits the shallow waters just off Qatar's coast, a person wading there could possibly step on one. The toxins in the stonefish's spine are strong enough to kill a person.

Stonefish have deadly venom.

Gulls are among the birds that live in Qatar throughout the year.

Many birds migrate through Qatar during the spring and autumn, and thus many Qataris enjoy bird-watching. Visiting birds include cormorants and flamingos. They rest along the shore, on the lush green lawns and in the trees that are cared for by people in Qatar's cities. The birds that live in Qatar year-round are mainly gulls and other seabirds, parakeets, and sparrows.

Animals and Sport

Three of Qatar's most beloved and traditional sporting events include animals: falconry, camel racing, and horse racing.

Falconry has a long tradition in Qatari culture. It began as a way for the Bedouin nomads to hunt the fast-flying bustard. Bustard meat added variety to the Bedouin diet. Today falconers compete in training their birds to swoop down and quickly capture their prey. The falconer follows the falcon on horseback or in a jeep to witness the attack.

Intelligent, obedient, and bold, falcons are excellent for hunting. Training usually takes about three weeks; a completely

Falconry is a traditional sport.

trained falcon will obey only its trainer. The falcons are lured out of the wild and then sold, usually for high prices. Though it was once a sport for commoners, today only the wealthy can afford to compete in the sport. It is quite popular with this segment of the population and is a part of Qatari culture that is centuries old.

Camel racing is a natural for a desert country like Qatar. Bedouins, of course, used camels for transport in the desert. Today four-wheel-drive vehicles make travel in the desert easier, and camels are mainly used in races. Races are usually held in the winter, and they are popular with tourists and locals alike.

Camel racing at Sheehaneya Race Track is fun to watch.

Camels

Camels played a major role in Qatar's history. Early residents of Qatar, the Bedouins, relied heavily on their camels to travel through the desert. The camels also carried goods and provided milk and meat. Bedouins gathered and wove camel hair for making tents, shoes, and other items. They dried camel skin to make leather tents and bags. Even camel manure had a use—when dried, it made good fuel for fires.

Camels are well suited for a desert environment. They can live on the pits of date palms and thorny desert shrubs. Their feet have two leathery, padded toes that spread out wide to walk on sand without sinking into it. Their humps are not filled with water, as many people mistakenly believe. Instead the humps are filled with fat, which the camel's body can use to create energy when no food and water are available. As a camel uses this fat, its hump gets smaller and slumps over. Camels can also close their eyes and nostrils tightly during a windstorm, keeping out even tiny grains of sand.

Horse racing is a popular Qatari sport. Members of the country's royalty are big supporters and participants. The Desert Marathon is a popular race that covers 26 miles (42 km) beginning at Ra's Laffan and ending at al-Ruways.

As if the desert climate weren't enough of a challenge for Qatar's plants and animals, humans have created even more. Many of these problems stem from the country's oil and natural-gas industry. Extensive growth of this industry is forcing animals out of their natural habitats. The oil and gas wells are prone to seepage, meaning that the petroleum and gas trickle out, polluting the surrounding land and water and killing the plant and animal life.

Mangrove plants along the coast have been especially exposed to such pollution. These tropical flowering trees and shrubs play an important role along the shore, where they grow in dense thickets in the muddy salt water. Their tangled masses of roots hold the sand in place. When they are gone, however, the tides can easily erode the coastline.

Traditional Qatari hunting practices have also threatened some animal species, driving them to the brink of extinction. Falconry, a sport that has been practiced for centuries, has diminished the numbers of the small birds caught by the falcons.

The government is working to reduce the environmental problems. It has established reserves for threatened animals. Each February 26 is Qatar Environment Day. Schoolchildren learn about caring for the natural world, planting trees, and picking up litter on this day. Some day it will be up to them to maintain the plants and animals that are part of Qatar's natural reserves.

CHAPTER

FOUR

History of the Peninsula

Q ATAR'S HISTORY AS AN INDEPENDENT NATION BEGAN ON September 1, 1971, only a few decades ago. However, human history in the region can be traced much further back. Archaeologists have found evidence that people moved into the area during the Old Stone Age, about 50,000 years ago. Rock engravings of animals and other figures show that hunters and fishermen lived along the coast of the peninsula by 5000 B.C. More archeological findings, including pottery fragments, tell us that about four thousand years ago a human society had begun to develop here as a part of the larger Southwest Asia region.

Opposite: **Ruins of an early al-Thani settlement, where Qatar's long-time ruling family once lived.**

Ancient pottery from an early Qatar civilization

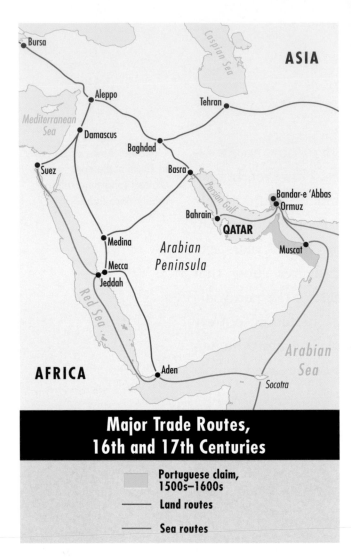

Major Trade Routes, 16th and 17th Centuries

Portuguese claim, 1500s–1600s

—— Land routes

—— Sea routes

Above right: **Vasco da Gama was the first European in the region.**

Not much is known about these people. Other civilizations left more traces of their presence and ways of life than the people of this little peninsula did. We do know that when Islam began to spread throughout the Middle East, beginning in A.D. 630, the people of Qatar accepted the new religion quite readily. We also know that they made their livings from the sea, mostly by fishing and collecting pearls to trade with neighboring settlements. They built fleets of ships to expand their trade. The ships also transported their army as it conquered new lands and converted people to Islam.

The Portuguese explorer Vasco da Gama sailed the first European ship into the Persian Gulf in 1498. During later centuries, the Persian Gulf became a major waterway linking the East and the West. The Portuguese established forts on the gulf's southern shore, where ships stopped en route to India and the Far East. Portuguese, Dutch, and British sailors traveled through the gulf regularly. Still, the small peninsula where Qatar is today was largely ignored by these travelers, as well as by the neighboring people of Persia, Turkey, and Oman, all of whom competed with one another for supremacy in the region.

Explorers to the Middle East, the Persian Gulf, and the Red Sea, c. 1502

Bedouins lived in desert camps, and were ready to move easily.

Pearl fishing was at the heart of Qatar's economy.

Most people on the quiet peninsula lived in small settlements on the east coast near Doha, then known as al-Bida. A few Bedouins lived in the desert interior, making a living by raising animals and growing date palms. But in 1766 skilled sailors and traders moved in from Kuwait, settling on the northwest coast near Zubara. These were the al-Khalifa and al-Jalahima tribes, and they helped the region develop into a major fishing port. The pearl trade grew as well, and the community became a major stopping point along the ocean trading route.

This replica depicts the strong Zubara settlement.

As the Zubara settlement grew stronger, its members began conquering other areas. The al-Khalifa tribe eventually took over Bahrain, about 30 miles (48 km) to the west, and made it their capital. Bahrain was one of the gulf's most important commercial centers, where goods such as spices, sugar, silk, and cloth from India were traded for pearls from Qatar. Zubara, though not as popular as Bahrain, also remained a major port.

The al-Jalahima tribe had helped the al-Khalifa tribe invade Bahrain, but soon after the two tribes began fighting. The al-Jalahima people believed that they didn't receive their fair share of goods from the country they had helped to conquer. They fled Bahrain, returning to their settlement,

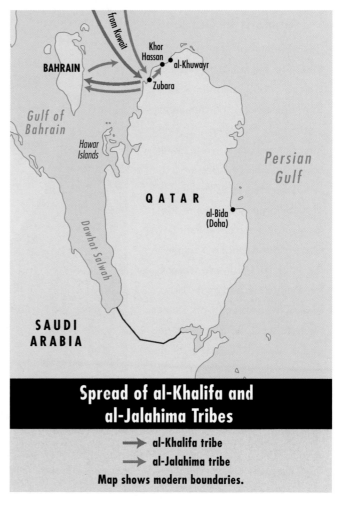

Spread of al-Khalifa and al-Jalahima Tribes

→ al-Khalifa tribe
→ al-Jalahima tribe
Map shows modern boundaries.

called Khor Hassan, in northern Qatar. There, two brothers, Abdullah and Rahmah bin Jabir, began feuding over who would take charge of the tribe. They were sons of the man who had originally led the tribe to Qatar. Eventually Abdullah left the country, and Rahmah, the younger brother, took charge.

While the tribes were fighting over who would control the land, Portugal was locked in a battle with Great Britain for

Tensions in Qatar

Descendants of the al-Khalifa tribe are still ruling Bahrain. In October 2002, Bahrain held its first democratic parliamentary election—a first step in giving Bahraini people a voice in the country's political process.

Conflict still exists between the al-Khalifa family and the al-Thani family, which took over the rule of Qatar after a lengthy struggle in the mid-1800s. More recently, tension has focused on the Hawar Islands, which lie just off Qatar's western coast. Both Bahrain and Qatar wanted ownership of the islands. In June 2001, the International Court of Justice at the Hague, the Netherlands, issued a ruling to which both sides agreed. Bahrain kept the main Hawar Island, but it dropped its claim to parts of Qatar's mainland. Qatar retained several important maritime areas

and their resources. This photo shows Bahraini Crown Prince Sheikh Salman bin Hamad al-Khalifa (left) greeted by Qatari Shaykh Jassim bin Hamad al-Thani in Doha in 2001.

control of the important Persian Gulf waterway. For decades, Portugal had charged levies, or fees, to other nations sailing ships in the gulf. In the early 1600s, the British arrived to change the system. The two nations battled over the gulf for centuries. Finally, in the 1800s, the British took control of the waterway to keep open its important trade route to India.

Trade ships faced plenty of dangers in these waters. Rahmah bin Jabir, known to be something of a pirate, was known for his cruelty. He invaded other ships, stole their cargo, and often killed their passengers. Members of the al-Khalifa tribe from Bahrain, old enemies of Rahmah's, were the target of his worst attacks.

Rahmah was eager to align with any other group who fought the al-Khalifa people. So when the Wahhabis, a faction of conservative Muslims, began to spread across the Middle East to promote their faith, Rahmah joined their cause. With their help, Rahmah increased his pirate attacks on al-Khalifa ships. The Wahhabis in turn established a stronghold in Qatar, and by 1809 they had control of the peninsula. As allegiances shifted throughout the gulf region in the following years, the Wahhabis turned on Rahmah. They ousted him from the country in 1816.

Throughout the 1800s, Qatar remained fairly isolated from the rest of the region. Principles of Wahhabism appealed to the various tribes throughout Qatar, including the al-Thani tribe, which embraced the religion. The al-Thanis had arrived on the peninsula during the eighteenth century and settled near Doha. The Wahhabi version of Islam grew in popularity,

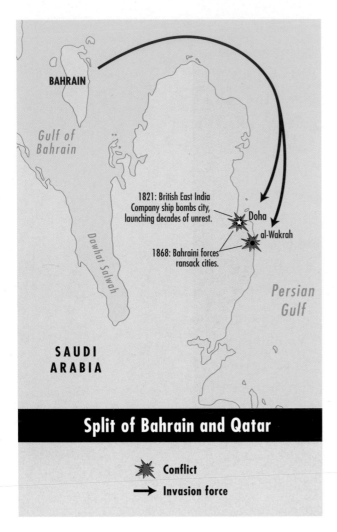

1821: British East India Company ship bombs city, launching decades of unrest.

Doha

al-Wakrah

1868: Bahraini forces ransack cities.

BAHRAIN

Gulf of Bahrain

Dawhat Salwah

SAUDI ARABIA

Persian Gulf

Split of Bahrain and Qatar

✴ Conflict

➡ Invasion force

and the al-Thani family became dominant in the peninsula.

As the al-Thani family and the Wahhabi religion gained power in Qatar, the British gained control of the gulf region. The General Treaty of Peace of 1820, signed by the British East India Company and the shaykhs of the coastal areas in the gulf, was accompanied by a series of agreements assuring that British ships would not be attacked by the shaykhs or their followers.

In 1821 a British East India Company ship bombed Doha. Hundreds of residents fled, and the town was destroyed. Unrest continued in the area for decades. Fighting was particularly fierce between the forces from Bahrain, led by the al-Khalifa tribe, and the Qatari forces, led by the al-Thani tribe. In 1868 a large group of warriors from Bahrain landed in Doha and al-Wakrah. They ransacked and looted the cities. When the British agent in the area, Colonel Lewis Pelly, learned of this fighting, he forced both sides into a peace treaty as a means of keeping the trade route open.

In the treaty, the British offered protection to the small Qatari peninsula in return for an agreement by residents to keep peace. This treaty marked the first time that Bahrain and

The al-Thani Dynasty

The al-Thani tribe arrived on the Qatari peninsula during the eighteenth century. They originally were members of the Tamim tribe that had settled along the southeastern coast near Doha. During the following decades, the al-Thani tribe spread along the eastern coast and settled in a number of small communities that their shaykhs controlled. They continued to gain power over the years. As the Wahhabi form of Islam, which the al-Thanis supported, spread through the land, their influence grew. In 1868, Britain's Colonel Lewis Pelly went to Shaykh Muhammad bin al-Thani to form an agreement not to engage in war at sea. With this action, the al-Thani family gained British recognition as the ruling family of Qatar.

Shaykh Muhammad maintained his capital city in al-Bida, which is now Doha, until his death in 1878. He was succeeded by his son, Shaykh Jassim bin Muhammad al-Thani, who was a very powerful ruler. At his death in 1913, his son, Shaykh Abdalla bin Jassim al-Thani, claimed power, and he ruled until 1949. Shaykh Ali bin Abdalla (right) became ruler after him.

In 1960, Ali bin Abdalla resigned. He was replaced by his son, Shaykh Hamad bin Ali al-Thani. But in 1972 his cousin, Shaykh Khalifa bin Hamad al-Thani, peacefully ousted Hamad bin Ali. Khalifa bin Hamad is considered the first modern ruler of Qatar. His son, Shaykh Hamad bin Khalifa al-Thani, succeeded him in a bloodless coup, or revolution, and became emir in 1995. This emir and his father made peace with one another the following year. Hamid bin Khalifa has appointed several of his brothers and sons to important posts within the government. The al-Thani family holds much political power throughout Qatar. Most consider them kind and wise rulers, and Qatari citizens are loyal to them.

Qatar were recognized as two distinct entities. Qatar had previously been considered a dependency of Bahrain. Qatar's Shaykh Muhammad bin al-Thani, who negotiated this treaty with Pelly, became even more influential as a result, and he advanced his family's importance. When he died in 1878, he was succeeded by his son, Shaykh Jassim bin Muhammad al-Thani, as Qatar's leader.

Jassim had a sharp mind and was skilled in making arrangements with other countries that allowed his country to remain independent. In addition to his treaty with the British, he was able to secure agreements with their enemies, the Ottomans of Turkey. When the Ottomans invaded the Qatari peninsula in 1893, Jassim allowed them to establish a base in Doha, but he made sure it remained small. In return he became a representative of the Ottoman sultan, or leader, and he grew in prominence throughout eastern Arabia. He reigned in Qatar until his death in 1913.

The Ottomans were allowed to keep their base in Doha after the emir's death. But in 1915, when the Ottoman army entered World War I on the side of Germany, the Ottomans were forced out of Doha. Turkey and Great Britain were on opposing sides in the war, and Great Britain controlled the rest of the gulf region. Though Qatar felt caught in the middle, it made sense to join Britain's cause. Once the Turks were ousted from Doha, Great Britain agreed to provide protection for Qatar. In return, Emir Abdalla bin Jassim al-Thani promised that Qatar would no longer deal with other foreign countries without Great Britain's approval.

Changes to the Economy

Until about 1920, Qatar's economy had been based on the pearl trade. But the bottom fell out of that market, and Qatar, never a wealthy country, grew even poorer. During the Great Depression of the 1930s, much of the rest of the world joined the United States in a severe economic slump. Qatar's food supply was disrupted, and people were going hungry. Disease spread rapidly throughout the country. People began fleeing Qatar for other parts of the gulf area, where there might be greater hope of survival.

For this reason, when oil prospectors arrived in Qatar in the mid-1930s, the emir welcomed them. They struck oil in 1939, but the oil industry did not fully begin to develop until 1949. During the interim, most of the world was focused on or involved in World War II. Eventually foreign oil companies realized the great resources available in Qatar and began investing heavily in the industry.

Once Qatar began exporting oil in 1949, its economy improved rapidly. But the money that began to flow into the country caused trouble for the

The first oil well in Qatar

aging emir, Abdalla bin Jassim. Several of his relatives threatened a bloody government overthrow if they did not receive larger "allowances" from the profits. The emir asked Great Britain for protection. He promised the British a greater role in ruling the nation as long as it supported the emir's son, Ali bin Abdalla, as he came into power in 1949.

The official presence of the British in Qatar helped improve government structures and build roads and hospitals. Qatar's first school opened in 1952. The nation had telephone service the next year, and in 1954 its first desalination plant provided fresh water for citizens. The emir and his family lived very well, even though the British held much of the political power in Qatar. Many members of the al-Thani family lived extravagant lives—and soon al-Thani family members who received less money, along with Qatari citizens in general, began to complain. The controversy caused Emir Ali bin Abdalla to resign in 1960, and his son, Hamad bin Ali, assumed power.

One of the new emir's first official actions was to increase funding to his family members and to give government positions to several of them. The public could take no more. Groups of low-level workers and others formed the National Unity Front and called a general strike throughout the country. Shaykh Hamad bin Ali jailed some of the strike leaders and sent others out of the country. But he did make some reforms. He granted land and loans to poor Qataris and spent money to diversify the country's economy by building a cement factory and improving farming practices.

In 1971, Great Britain announced it was leaving the region. Qatar initiated an agreement with Bahrain and the Trucial States, now called the United Arab Emirates. But the talks broke down when Bahrain rejected the idea of a union. Qatar declared its independence on September 1, 1971. Shortly after, the emir's cousin, Khalifa bin Hamad al-Thani, seized control of the country during a coup that occurred while the emir was out of the country, hunting with falcons in Iran.

Shaykh Khalifa bin Hamad al-Thani and British Foreign Secretary Sir Alec Douglas-Home in 1971

The new emir brought stability to Qatar. He reduced the amount of money going to family members and spent more on social programs—health care, education, and housing—for the people of Qatar. In 1974 oil prices around the world rose sharply, and Qatar became prosperous once more. The emir used much of the money to provide free services, such as education and health care, to the Qatari people.

Emir Khalifa bin Hamad has been called the first modern ruler of Qatar. Even as the country was becoming more modern, however, the emir emphasized traditional Wahhabi Muslim values and customs. Regular daily prayers, prohibition of alcohol, and wearing conservative clothing remained important religious laws in Qatar.

Qatar's foreign policy usually followed the lead of its large neighbor, Saudi Arabia, though not always. Saudi Arabia joined the United States in the first Gulf War in 1990–91. Qatar, though, sought closer ties with Iran and began a diplomatic and economic relationship with Israel.

Many of these decisions were guided by the emir's son, Shaykh Hamad bin Khalifa al-Thani, who had been allowed to take over much of the governing duties of the country. But he disagreed with his father over the country's great oil wealth. When he forced his father out of office in 1995, the emir fought back with a lengthy lawsuit. Eventually the two came to a peaceful resolution.

Today the emir is continuing to modernize Qatar. He is striving to bring democracy, greater rights for women, and more freedom of the press to Qatar.

Shayka Mouza bint Nasser al-Misnad

One of the strongest forces for advancing women's rights in Qatar is Shayka Mouza bint Nasser al-Misnad. She is the second wife of the current emir, Shaykh Hamad bin Khalifa al-Thani, and has been first lady of the country since 1998. The shayka has been a strong supporter of a larger role for women in politics. Thanks in large part to her efforts, women accounted for 44 percent of all voters in the 1999 elections in Qatar, and six women ran for public office. They were the first women ever to run for office in a gulf nation. Though they didn't win offices, these candidates opened the door to greater political participation for women.

Education for women is also gaining ground in Qatar. The shayka is the director of the new Education City in Doha, which is bringing satellite campuses of major U.S. universities to Qatar. Many students are women. At the University of Qatar, where the shayka's aunt is a vice president, more than two-thirds of the nine thousand students are female.

Shayka Mouza and her husband, Shaykh Hamad, have worked together to grant a level of freedom to women that is rarely seen in the Arab world.

CHAPTER FIVE

Dynasties and Democracy

Hamad bin Khalifa Al-Thani is a big fan of youth sports. He believes that sports play an important role in helping young people learn to be better citizens. He has given sports programs much support. His Highness Shaykh Hamad bin Khalifa al-Thani, Emir of the State of Qatar, knew that he would someday be a ruler, even back in the days when he himself was a youngster playing sports.

Qatar is ruled by a traditional monarchy—that is, a government led by a single ruler. Qatar's ruler is the emir. The al-Thani family has held power since the mid-1800s. The kingship has passed from father to son, when the father dies or resigns from his role. If a ruler had no son, he chose another male relative, perhaps a brother or a nephew, from within the family. The person next in line to assume power while another rules is called the heir apparent and has various official duties.

Opposite: **Emiri Diwan, the royal palace in Doha**

The Constitution

As Qatar has developed and matured as an independent country, its constitution has changed with it. The first Qatari constitution was written in 1970, even before the nation was independent. It was revised in 1972 to meet the country's new responsibilities. Since then, international politics and allegiances in the Persian Gulf and other parts of the Arab world have shifted, and the Qatari constitution has been amended through the years to accommodate the new political situations.

The Current Emir

His Highness Shaykh Hamad bin Khalifa al-Thani (below) has been emir since June 27, 1995. Born in 1952, he was educated in Qatari schools and graduated from the Royal Military Academy in 1971. He

was eventually appointed Commander-in-Chief of the Qatari Armed Forces. In that position, he focused on updating the military, providing troops with state-of-the-art weapons. He became heir apparent in 1977 and took on several leadership roles, one of which was heading the Higher Council for Youth Welfare. In this position, he worked to increase and improve sporting programs for the young people of Qatar.

As emir, one of Hamad bin Khalifa's major focuses has been boosting Qatar's relations with countries throughout the world. In the process, he has received medals and honors from such countries as France, Pakistan, Germany, Romania, Italy, Yemen, and Cuba. He has also made great strides toward modernizing the country and granting its citizens more rights. Most Qatari people see him as tolerant and fair.

The heir apparent is His Highness Shaykh Tamim bin Hamad al-Thani (below). Born in Doha in 1979, he is the emir's fourth son, and he became heir apparent in 2003. He is involved in environmental protection, public services, and development of the armed forces. He also heads Qatar's Olympic committee.

One of the most important changes for the country occurred in 1999, when Qatar held free elections for the first time in its history. While a monarchy still rules the country at its national level, the elections represented a move toward democracy at the local level. Women were allowed to vote and were encouraged to run for office.

Even though the Qatari constitution has changed, at its heart it remains the same. It states that Qatar is an independent Arab state; Islam is its official religion; and the Sharia, or Islamic law, is the basis for legislation in the country. Arabic is its official language.

The government maintains the country's security and stability and is responsible for defending its people against any act of aggression. Qatar also supports the unity of Arab nations. This unity, the monarchy believes, is necessary because of the common interests of the region and of the Arab world. Qatar's international policy also calls for strengthening

Qatar's first free elections were held in 1999, and women and men were both able to vote.

Government buildings in Doha.

friendly relations with all countries, particularly with other Islamic nations.

The government controls and supervises Qatar's economy, but individuals are allowed private ownership of businesses and wealth, according to the constitution. All free enterprise is guaranteed, as long it does not conflict with the interests of the country. The government is also responsible for providing public jobs for all citizens.

The monarchy supports families as the nucleus of society. Laws ensure that the family unit is protected and that young people are provided for. All Qataris have equal civil rights under the law, and one may not discriminate against others based on religion or race. A person charged with a crime has the right to a fair trial and is considered to be innocent until proven guilty.

Role of the Emir

The emir holds both legislative and executive powers, meaning that he is responsible for creating laws and government practices in Qatar and for seeing that the laws and practices are carried out. He is assisted in his legislative duties by a prime minister and a Council of Ministers, each of whom are

Qatari foreign minister Shaykh Hamad bin Jassem al-Thani and U.S. defense secretary Donald Rumsfeld signing a new military treaty in December 2002.

Prime minister Abdalla bin Khalifa al-Thani

responsible for a different aspect of government. A separate Advisory Council offers recommendations and advice on public matters.

Members of the Council of Ministers are appointed by the emir, who also accepts any member resignation. This council helps to create and enforce laws, monitors government finances, and drafts the country's budget. The current prime minister is His Highness Shaykh Abdalla bin Khalifa al-Thani, brother of the current emir.

Though the emir and the Council of Ministers write the laws, Qatari regulations state that no law may be enacted until the Advisory Council has

NATIONAL GOVERNMENT OF QATAR

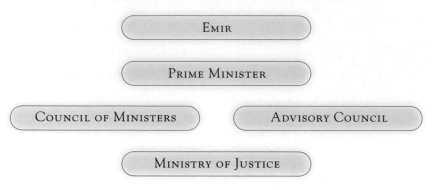

discussed and recommended it. This council has thirty-five members, all appointed by the emir. Members are selected on the basis of their reputation for sound judgment. Their goal is to oversee the country's development and to ensure that any changes are for the good of its citizens.

The Flag of Qatar

The national flag of Qatar is maroon with a wide stripe of white along the left side. The two colors join in a serrated line. White represents peace; maroon symbolizes the blood shed during the wars Qatar has endured. The serrated line has nine points, symbolizing that Qatar was the ninth emirate in the Persian Gulf following the Qatari-British treaty in 1916.

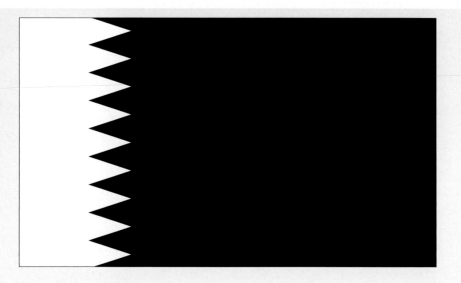

Qatar's Justice System

Qatar's Ministry of Justice oversees the civil judiciary. This judiciary is, according to the nation's constitution, an independent authority, meaning that judges are allowed to make decisions on their own. The legal system in the country is Sharia Judiciary. It is based on Islamic law, and judges use these principles to decide on the cases they hear. Sharia courts hear cases relating to Muslims and decide them based on teachings set down in the Qur'an.

The Military

Qatar maintains a relatively small military of about 12,400 men. Most are in the nation's army, but Qatar also has a navy, an air force, and a public security force. The cost of maintaining the military forces accounts for about 11 percent of the

The National Anthem

Qatar's national anthem was adopted in 1996, shortly after the new emir took the throne. Abdul Aziz Nasser composed the music. It is called "Al-Salam al-Amiri," or "The Amiri Anthem."

The lyrics, in English, are:
Swearing by God who erected the sky
Swearing by God who spread the light
Qatar will always be free
Sublimed by the souls of the sincere
Proceed thou on the manners of the ascendants
And advance on the Prophet's guidance.
In my heart,
Qatar is an epic of glory and dignity
Qatar is land of the early men
Who protect us at time of distress,
Doves they can be at times of peace,
Warriors they are at times of sacrifice.

Qatar's military is small, but plays an important role in the Persian Gulf region.

country's spending. Qatar's military forces played an important role in supporting U.S. military forces during the Gulf War in 1991 and the U.S. invasion of Iraq in 2003. Great Britain and France, along with the United States, have signed defense pacts with Qatar, which is a member of the Gulf Cooperation Council. This is a collective defense arrangement among the member countries of Saudi Arabia, Kuwait, Bahrain, the United Arab Emirates, and Oman.

International Relations

Qatar is moving quickly toward modernization and democracy, and thus its relations with other nations are in transition. It remains a conservative Muslim nation and an important part of the Arab world. The country's ties to the people of other Middle Eastern nations are strong—they all share a history and a religion, as well as similar values and customs.

At the same time, Qatar is forging a relationship with the United States and other Western nations—an important step in becoming more democratic. It also aims to improve its technology and economy. In 2003, when the United States went to war against Iraqi leader Saddam Hussein, Qatar became one of America's most strategic allies. Thousands of U.S. troops were based in Qatar as a staging point for their Iraqi operations.

Qatar's alliance with the United States threw it into conflict with some of its neighbors, most of whom opposed the U.S. invasion of Iraq. Not all Qataris were happy about the alliance either. Qatari leaders point out, however, that many Persian Gulf nations have maintained friendly relations with the United States over the years, including Kuwait and Oman.

Following the overthrow of Saddam Hussein, Qatar's Shaykh Hamad bin Khalifa al-Thani supported the U.S. decision to keep armed forces in Iraq while that country strives to become a democracy. It is important, the shaykh said, that the United States help Iraq establish democratic principles of government.

U.S. President George Bush visiting U.S. military at Camp al-Sayliyah in June 2003.

Qatar also needs the security of the American troops that defend it, Qatari officials say, since it is a small country in the middle of a politically volatile region. During the 1991 Gulf War, some citizens felt that they had no strong military to protect them or to safeguard the country's energy resources and investments in oil and gas production. Others argued that Qatar is not a target of any other Middle Eastern country unless its foreign policies anger other Arab nations.

Qatari leaders also contend that the country's alliance with the United States extends well beyond a military effort. Satellite campuses of several major American universities are already based in Doha, and more are planned. The Qatari government is striving to develop a strong reputation for higher education. The government insists that this is the main focus of Qatar's relationship with the United States.

Doha: Did You Know This?

Qatar's capital is the city of Doha. Its population is 318,500. Including the nearby city of al-Rayyān, which has 194,800 residents, this area of the country is home to more than 80 percent of Qatar's population. Doha was a small fishing village until the eighteenth century, when it became the nation's capital. The previous capital had been Zubara, in the northwest part of the country. In the nineteenth century, the al-Thani family took up headquarters in Doha. They became the ruling family of Qatar, and the city became far more important and powerful than it had been.

Doha's population boom has been most prominent, though, in the most recent decades, when the country's oil boom brought thousands of people to the city from other parts of Qatar and other parts of the world. The city limits continue to radiate north, south, and west from its center along the coast. It's a well-planned city, with major roads forming ever-larger arcs around the bay. Though trees and shrubs don't grow here naturally, great care has been taken to plant and maintain vegetation. Doha has plenty of green, with many parks and lovely boulevards.

Doha is the hub of the country's government, of course, but it is also its communication center. The country's main seaport is here—a large, manmade deep-water port that opened in 1969. The country's only commercial airport is here, as are most of Qatar's tourist attractions and sports facilities. Only Qatar's oil and natural-gas industries are not headquartered here.

The corniche is a popular spot in the heart of Doha. This coastal path, with its cooling shade trees, curves in a 5-mile (8-km) arc along the bay. Many people enjoy

taking a pleasant stroll, jogging, or bike riding here. It's also a nice spot for workers to sit during lunchtime. Many important buildings line this pathway, including several government ministry buildings, and the royal palace. The National Museum, a highlight attraction in Doha, is also located along the corniche. Fine examples of old architecture are preserved within the museum. The Qatar National Theater and some of the city's major hotels are also on the corniche (top right).

Doha has plenty to see elsewhere, too. The Doha Zoo contains a large variety of animals. The University of Qatar, built in 1973, and several other interesting museums lie within the city's borders.

The old *souq*, or traditional Middle Eastern market, is a busy place in Doha. It bustles with sellers and buyers eager to find the best deals on kitchenware, watches, spices, tools, and leather items. At a gold souq, jewelry sellers offer beautiful gold bracelets, earrings, chains, and rings. Vendors sell food products at the fruit and vegetable souq and the meat and fish souq. Those who prefer modern shopping malls over souqs can find plenty of these in Doha as well.

Population: 318,500

Average daily temperature: 104°F (40°C) in the summer, and 68°F (20°C) in the winter

Average annual rainfall: less than 2 inches (5 cm)

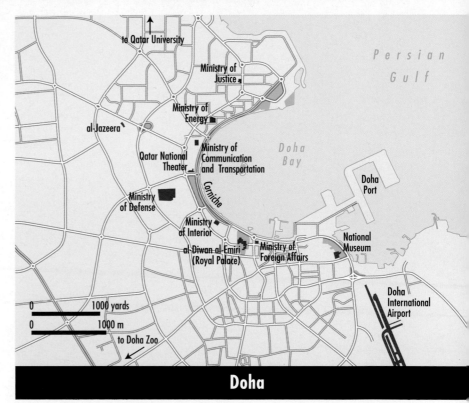

Doha

CHAPTER

SIX

From Pearls
to Petroleum

THE DESERT ENVIRONMENT OF QATAR DOESN'T LOOK LIKE much more than a lot of sand and dust. But deep underground is a substance that supports much of the activity above ground: oil!

Oil was discovered in Qatar in 1939. At that time, Qatar was a poor nation that had been dependent on a pearl trade and the fishing industry. As Qatar's oil production increased over the years, so did its wealth. Oil production has helped the country pay for schools, hospitals, roads, and ports. It has helped families pay for food, shelter, and clothing. The people of Qatar are on average among the world's wealthiest, thanks to the strength of the country's oil reserves.

Opposite: **Qatar's oil industry, including this refinery, is owned by the government.**

Petroleum Wealth

Qatar's income relies heavily on petroleum production and export. The government controls the oil and gas industry through Qatar Petroleum, which is owned by the state. Established in 1974, Qatar Petroleum is responsible for all aspects of the country's petroleum business. Oil and gas production make up more than 66 percent of Qatar's national revenue (the amount of money the country earns). Oil brings in about 80 percent of the country's export income and provides about 66 percent of the money that funds the government itself.

Oil storage near Umm Said. The oil industry is a major part of Qatar's economy.

In 2002 the finance minister of Qatar estimated that by 2005, Qataris would enjoy the highest per capita (per person) income in the world. When he made this prediction, the nation's per capita income was comparable to US $21,200. Only the European nations of Switzerland and Luxembourg had higher per capita incomes.

This prediction is supported by the $150 million budget surplus that Qatar maintained in 2002. Its healthy gas and oil reserves mean that the nation should remain prosperous for many years.

Oil

Most of Qatar's oil production is based in the west, around Dukhān, with three offshore oil fields and one field on land. The onshore field is the largest, supplying about half of the country's crude oil. Production began here in 1949, and with reserves of about 3.7 billion barrels, it should continue until about 2025, if output remains about the same as it is now.

The offshore oil fields began production in 1964. These fields are located in waters on the eastern side of the peninsula.

One of three offshore oil fields.

Exploration work is in progress to see whether oil lies off the country's western shore too. Some of Qatar's offshore fields are operated solely by Qatar Petroleum; others are operated by a joint effort of Qatar Petroleum and foreign petroleum companies.

Much of Qatar's crude oil is transported across the country to Messaieed in pipelines that run above the desert landscape. From Messaieed the crude oil is exported by ship to countries throughout the world. The countries that purchase most of Qatar's crude oil are Japan, Thailand, and Singapore. Other trading partners include the United States and the United Kingdom.

Oil pipeline from Dukhān to Umm Said. From there, the oil will be shipped around the world.

Natural Gas

Natural gas is another important part of the Qatar economy. In some places, natural gas is mixed in with crude oil in the same reserves. This is called associated gas. In other areas, it

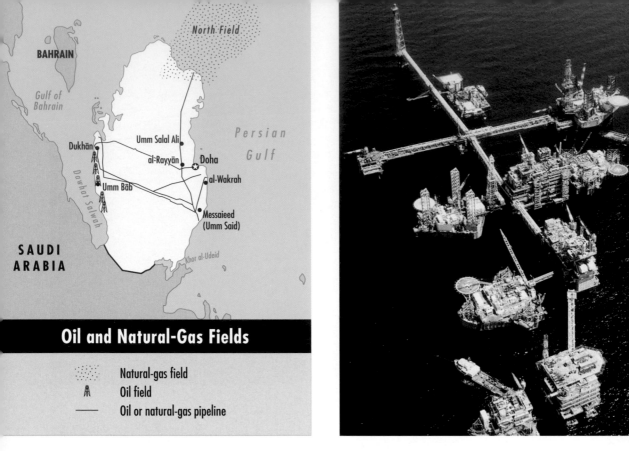

Oil and Natural-Gas Fields

Natural-gas field

Oil field

Oil or natural-gas pipeline

Above right: **The North Field is the largest natural gas field of its type.**

occurs alone. This is called nonassociated natural gas. Both types are found in Qatar. Natural-gas reserves were discovered in Qatar in 1963, and production has rapidly increased since a large offshore gas field was discovered in Qatari territory in the early 1980s. The North Field, as it is called, is just off the northern tip of the Qatari peninsula, extending about 100 miles (161 km) into the gulf. It is the largest nonassociated natural-gas field in the world.

In total, at least 8.5 trillion cubic feet of natural gas is held in reserve in Qatar. This is the third-largest reserve in the world; only Russia and Iran have bigger reserves. The Qatari government is investing in natural gas by building more production facilities. The country now produces about

783,000 barrels a day, and this amount is expected to increase during the next decade and bring greater income to the Qatar economy.

Production of Qatar's natural-gas resources has grown more slowly than oil production because natural gas is far more difficult to export. Either it must be transported through massive pipelines built just for that purpose, or it must first be converted into liquefied natural gas. This process requires high pressure and extremely low temperatures. When the gas turns to liquid, it takes up much less space than in its gas form, so it is much more practical and economical to transport.

Weights and Measures

Qatar uses the metric system of weights and measures. The basic unit of distance is the meter, the basic unit of weight is the gram, and the basic unit of liquid measure is the liter.

A liquid-gas tanker takes Qatar's natural gas to distant ports.

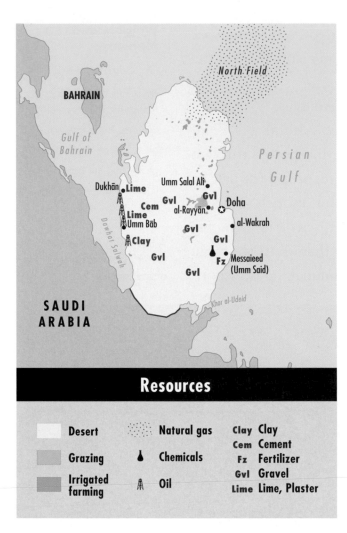

Resources

Desert	Natural gas	Clay	Clay
Grazing	Chemicals	Cem	Cement
Irrigated farming	Oil	Fz	Fertilizer
		Gvl	Gravel
		Lime	Lime, Plaster

The liquefied natural gas is shipped out in special tankers. This is the method used by Qatar when it exports natural gas to distant countries, including Japan, South Korea, India, and Spain. The country also sells natural gas by pipeline to the nearby nations of United Arab Emirates and Oman.

A Government-Run Economy

The Qatari government not only owns the country's petroleum business, but it also owns the nation's farmlands and many manufacturing facilities. In fact, the government manages nearly all of the country's economic activities. Officials are trying to diversify the nation's economy by increasing revenue from industries and businesses other than oil. By doing so, they hope to keep the economy fairly stable no matter what the demand for oil and gas may be. The government also wants to prepare for the time when the oil reserves may become depleted.

A few other industries contribute to Qatar's economy. Most industrial activity is centered around the city of Messaieed, which has cement and fertilizer manufacturers and

---

What Qatar Grows, Makes, and Mines

Agriculture

Vegetables (2001 est.)	55,600 metric tons
Fruits (2001 est.)	23,000 metric tons
All Meats	14,000 metric tons
Cereals	6,000 metric tons

Manufacturing (2001 est.)

Cement	1 billion metric tons
Steel	907,000 metric tons
Urea (Fertilizer)	748,000 metric tons

Mining

Crude Oil (2001 est.)	227 billion barrels
Natural Gas (2001 est.)	37 billion cubic meters
Sulfur	65 million metric tons
Limestone	900,000 metric tons

---

steel producers. Of these, the most profitable has been the steel industry, which mainly produces the reinforcing bars commonly used in construction.

Though the government owns most Qatari businesses, the country also has the Doha Securities Market, where stocks are bought and sold. Foreign business investment is welcomed. The Qatari government has successfully attracted investment in the country's petroleum industry. Foreigners are encouraged to invest in other areas of the economy as well, and they are permitted to own businesses in Qatar. However, laws limit the amount of property they may own.

It's necessary to irrigate crops in Qatar.

Agriculture

Agriculture makes up only about 2 percent of Qatar's income. The soil and water resources needed to grow crops well are in short supply in this desert country. Farmers use treated sewage water and desalinated water to irrigate crops in some areas of the country.

Qatari farmers grow enough fruits and vegetables—especially cereal grains, squash, tomatoes, and eggplant—to provide for about half of the country's needs. They also raise animals, including about 15,000 cattle, 50,000 camels, 79,000 goats, 4 million chickens, and almost 215,000 sheep annually. Fishermen haul in about 7,142 metric tons of seafood, mainly shrimp, each year.

These sheep at the market will provide both wool and meat.

Tourists enjoy camel rides.

Tourism

Qatar hopes to bring more foreigners into the country as tourists. The largest shopping center in the Middle East recently opened in Doha, and the 2006 Asian Games will be held in Qatar.

The country's historic sites, including many ancient castles and forts, also lure tourists to Qatar. One historic site is Jebel al-Jassasiya, a fascinating place on Qatar's hilly northeastern coast. Thousands of years ago, residents carved pictures into the stone, and many people now travel there to see the interesting engravings. Nearby beaches offer another reason to visit. Though Qatar is not yet a major tourist destination, the country's history and natural resources make it a promising region.

Living in a Wealthy Land

No real unemployment exists in Qatar, because nearly all Qataris who wish to work are able to get a job. Laws require businesses to give preference to Qataris, then to other Arabs, and then finally to other foreigners when hiring. Even with these restrictions, most of the workers in the country are from outside Qatar, since the Qatari population cannot provide enough workers.

The Pearl Trade

Nineteenth-century Qataris believed that a pearl was simply a drop of dew that an oyster took in when it rose to the top of the sea at night. The lives of the Qataris who believed this myth depended upon pearls. After Europeans arrived in the gulf in the 1800s, the slave trade was forbidden, European ships that were larger than the dhows Arabs sailed took over the shipping business, and piracy was no longer profitable. Little was left for Qataris to make a living except fishing and pearling.

The pearl trade grew, however, thanks to the European presence in the gulf. The peace that the British helped establish made it easier to obtain pearls. The trade continued to grow until it reached its peak in the years just before World War I. Fashionable women throughout Europe and North America created an enormous demand for pearl jewelry.

Pearling was a hard life. Divers attached stones to their feet to help them reach deeper waters, and they stayed underwater for as long as two minutes at a time, holding their breath while searching for oysters. Sharks and poisonous fish swam the waters, so the work was dangerous. But it was the best living available in Qatar, and pearling kept the economy alive.

When the Great Depression hit in the 1930s, the demand for pearls dropped. At the same time, the Japanese developed a technique for creating cultured pearls. They placed a grain of sand in each oyster so that the oyster would grow a pearl around it as protection. These types of pearls were cheaper to buy than natural pearls from the gulf. Qatar, always a poor country, slid into serious decline when its pearl trade died. Qataris didn't know it then, but the oil industry would eventually revive their economy and bring the country great wealth. Unfortunately, they would endure nearly two decades of poverty before that happened.

The Qatari Work Day

People in Qatar usually begin the workday early, while the temperature is still fairly low. Most are in their shops and offices by 7 A.M. They work until noon, and then usually take several hours off during the hottest part of the day. They return to work from 4 until about 7 P.M.

The workweek runs from Saturday through Wednesday in Qatar, and Thursday and Friday are "weekend" days, when many Qataris have time off from their jobs. This is when they relax and usually spend time with their families.

The government encourages Qataris to join the industrial work force, but foreigners fill most jobs. The majority of Qatari citizens work in the service sector. Women make up only 15 percent of the work force. For many years, cultural restriction discouraged women from working. Today, however, the government is striving to get more women to work, and the effort

Women at work at
television station Al-Jazeera

is beginning to make a difference. There are more women than men in Qatar universities, and it is likely that many of these educated women will enter the work force. Most working women today are employed as clerks, nurses, and teachers.

Qatari Currency

The basic unit of currency in Qatar is the Qatari riyal. One Qatari riyal is equal to 100 dirhams. One U.S. dollar equals 3.64 riyals. This is a fixed rate. Riyals come in a variety of denominations. On some bills, a dhow (the traditional sailing boat), is pictured, along with swords and a palm tree. Oil derricks in the Persian Gulf, part of the backbone of Qatar's economy, are depicted on other bills.

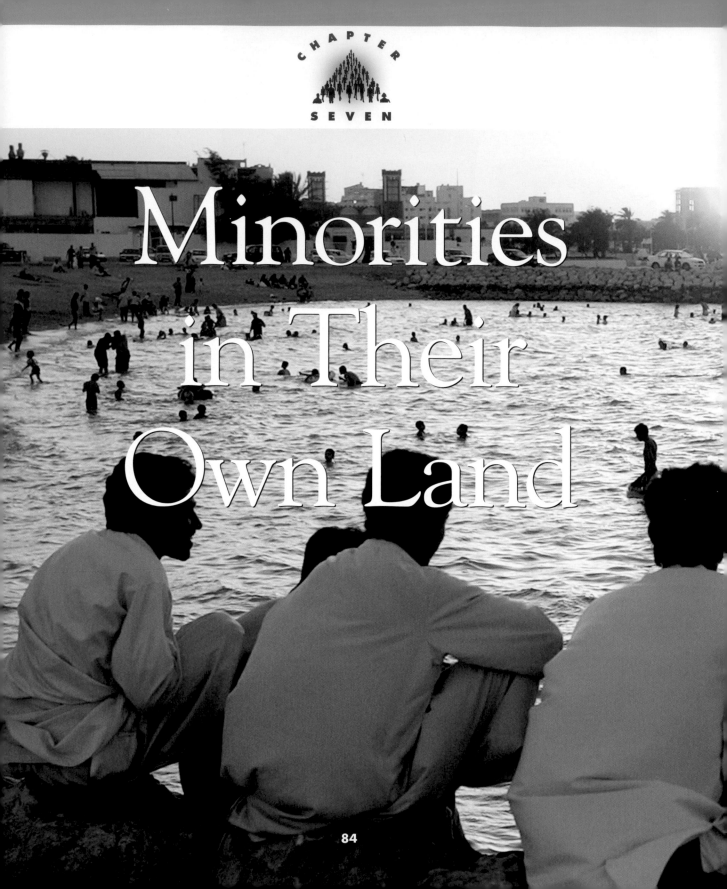

Minorities in Their Own Land

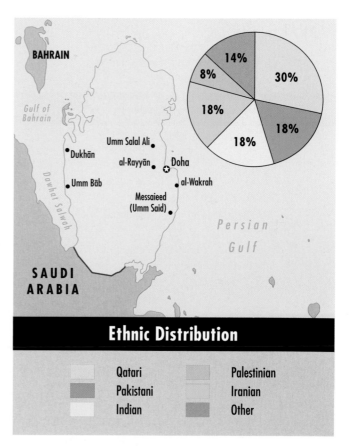

ᴺATIVE Qᴀᴛᴀʀɪꜱ ᴀʀᴇ ᴀ ᴍɪɴᴏʀɪᴛʏ ɪɴ ᴛʜᴇɪʀ ᴏᴡɴ ᴄᴏᴜɴ-try. They make up only about 30 percent of the population. Most natives are of Najdi descent, meaning that their ancestors were from migratory tribes coming from northwestern Saudi Arabia during the eighteenth century. A few native Qataris are descended from members of Omani tribes as well.

About 70 percent of Qatar residents are not native Qataris. Many of the foreigners living in Qatar are expatriates from Pakistan, India, Palestine, and Iran. Others have come to Qatar from Syria, Jordan, and Lebanon. British citizens live in Qatar as well. Most have temporary residency status and came to Qatar to work in the oil industry.

Opposite: **A beach in Doha draws many people eager to cool off.**

The Ethnic Breakdown of Qatar's Population

Qatari	30 %
Pakistani	18 %
Indian	18 %
Iranian	18 %
Palestinian	8 %
Other, including Syrian, Jordanian, Lebanese, and British	14 %

Ethnic Distribution

Qatari		Palestinian	
Pakistani		Iranian	
Indian		Other	

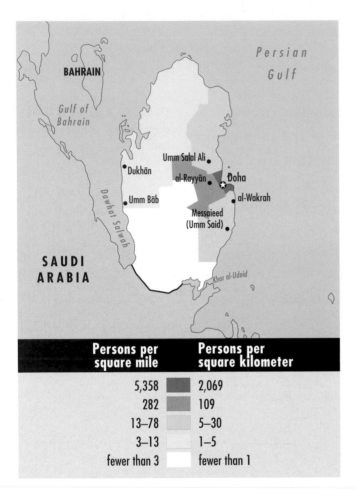

Persons per square mile		Persons per square kilometer
5,358		2,069
282		109
13–78		5–30
3–13		1–5
fewer than 3		fewer than 1

Although the percentage of Qatari citizens is low within their own country, Qataris nonetheless maintain a strong sense of culture and tradition. Much of Qatar's history and customs have been preserved for generations. Ancient values that include offering gracious hospitality to guests and generosity to strangers are still practiced today. Many of these values have been passed on orally; until recently few Qataris knew how to read. Still, most natives know history and the stories of their holy book, the Qur'an, almost word for word.

Qatari fishers, pearlers, and cattle herders learned important values. They appreciated the importance of hard work, patience, loyalty, and resourcefulness. Though few Qataris are fishers, pearlers, or cattle herders today, these qualities are still important.

Many modern Qataris have moved to Doha and other cities to find good jobs. They work in offices, stores, or other professions. Each weekend many head home to their families and friends in the villages where they grew up.

Children are the highlight of Arab families. Most parents like to indulge their children and often take keen interest in the children of their friends and relatives. Most families spend much time together; even extended families often gather for meals and celebrations. Arabic people are typically very warm toward outsiders too. They will often invite friends to join in family get-togethers.

Boys on a dhow. Family life revolves around children.

Qataris are very warm, friendly people. These young men exchange a traditional greeting.

Outside of family events, men and women in Qatar rarely socialize together or mix during daily activities. They usually pray in separate places, use different areas of government offices, and shop at different stores. Wealthy families have rooms called *majlis* in their homes. Here men receive their male guests. In other rooms, only women gather.

A Qatari male would never shake the hand of a Qatari female, although men shake hands with one another when they meet. Visitors, especially those who are left-handed, should remember that the right hand and never the left is used for shaking hands and for eating. When close friends of the same sex meet or walk together, they often link arms or hold hands. But Qataris are careful when seated to avoid showing the soles of their shoes to others. This is considered very rude.

Names and Families

Tribes—which are essentially large extended families—are the basic unit of society in Qatar and throughout the rest of the Persian Gulf region. Within tribes are clans, which are further divided into households. Business is often conducted within tribes, and marriages are often arranged between tribal members. People of the same tribe tend to live near one another, and they share many customs. At one time, all members of each tribe wore similar styles of clothing, although this is not usually the case today.

Family names are often taken from those of important leaders throughout Middle Eastern history. That is why the name Mahmoud, taken from the religious leader Muhammad, is quite common. Al-Thani, taken from the name of the ruling family of Qatar, is also popular. Male names always incorporate the term *bin*, which means "son of," followed by the father's name. This reflects the importance of family identification. Likewise, daughters use the term *bint*, or "daughter of," in their names, followed by the name of their father.

Bedouin People

The Bedouin people have lived in the deserts of the Middle East for centuries. They are nomads, meaning that they follow a way of life that takes them from place to place in the desert in search of food and water. They bring their herds of camels, sheep, and goats with them. The animals eventually are taken to market to be sold for meat. This has been the traditional lifestyle followed by most Qataris for centuries.

Bedouin camel herder in desert camp

Most Bedouin people today no longer follow this way of life. Many have moved to cities to find jobs and an easier way of life. Other Bedouins have remained in the desert, but they move about in motorized vehicles. Only a few still live as their ancestors did centuries ago. Their homes are large tents made of woven goat and camel hair. Supported by only a few poles, the tents are easy to set up and to take down. They keep people warm in the cool desert winters and also provide shade from the hot summer sun, allowing breezes to pass through their sides.

Bedouins usually travel together in groups of several families, but each family pitches its tents far away from other families for privacy. They tend to keep to themselves, yet they recognize the importance of depending upon others. The desert is huge and isolated, and each person needs others to help in difficult times. It is an ancient lifestyle, common to only a few Bedouins today.

These tents are easy to move.

Arabic is the main language of Qatar.

Qataris mainly speak Arabic, although English and other languages are frequently spoken as well. A large Qatari population of Pakistani citizens speak their native language, Urdu, in addition to Arabic.

Arabic has several dialects. Modern standard Arabic is the formal, literary version. It is what children learn in school and is the dialect used in newspapers throughout the Arab world. Arabs of different nations can easily communicate using this language. Spoken Arabic, however, is almost always a local dialect, with variations of pronunciations and words. These slight differences can sometimes cause problems in communication. Classical Arabic is another form of the language, and although it's no longer spoken very often, it is the language of the Qur'an.

It is nearly impossible to record Arabic words using the Roman alphabet common to English-speaking people. This is because there are sounds in Arabic that cannot be represented by Roman letters. One sound, for example, is formed deep in the throat by pushing air out while tightening the throat muscles. Another sound is a deep, fast breathing sound, similar to the noise made when people blow on their eyeglasses to clean them. Several methods of writing have been devised to try to re-create the sounds of the Arabic words, but none are perfect. That's why you often see several different spellings of common Arabic terms. Islam's holy book may be spelled Qur'an or

Koran, for example, and the name of the Prophet of Islam may be spelled Mohammed or Muhammad.

Written Arabic reads from right to left, in the opposite direction of the way we read in English. The letters are all cursive; each letter in a word connects in a flowing style to those around it. The Arabic alphabet has twenty-eight letters, all of them consonants. Three vowel sounds are represented by symbols written above or below the letters. Each letter is written in a slightly different way depending on whether it comes at the beginning, middle, or end of a word.

Each written letter has its own distinct sound—unlike English, in which some letters sound different depending upon the other letters with which they are paired. An example of this is the sound of *t* versus *th*. Many English speakers view Arabic as difficult to read. In fact, it has been classified by the U.S. government as the second most difficult foreign language to learn. Only Chinese is considered more difficult.

Common Arab Words and Terms

Arabic	English
as-saláamu :alái-kum	Hello (literally, "Peace be with you")
wa :alái-kum as-saláam	reply to "hello"
al-Hámdu li-l-láah	Praise be to God
Sabáah al-kháir	Good morning
Sabáah an-núur	Reply to "good morning"
Masáa' al-kháir	Good evening
Masáa an-núur	Reply to "good evening"
Shukran	Thank you
Má:a l-ásaf	I am sorry

Sample of Arabic writing

Minorities in Their Own Land **93**

A Nation of Muslims

LIFE FOR QATARI CITIZENS REVOLVES AROUND ISLAM, THE nation's official religion. Nearly all native residents are Muslims, or followers of Islam. The word "Islam" is taken from the Arabic word *aslama*, which means submission or surrender to God's will. Muslims in Qatar and other nations "surrender" to the teachings of Islam. Many of their daily activities, their frequent prayers, the respect they show to others, and their kind actions are a means of putting their faith into action.

Opposite: **Qur'an extract**

Although nearly all Qataris follow the Wahhabi version of Sunni Islam, others living in the country are free to observe their own faiths. Many Iranians living in Qatar are Shi'ite Muslims, while some of the Indians are Hindus or Christians. Most of the Europeans and Filipinos living in Qatar are Christian.

Religious Distribution of Qatari People	
Muslim	93%
Christian	6%
Hindu	0.8%
Baha'i	0.2%

The History of Islam

The prophet Muhammad founded Islam in the A.D. 600s. He was born in A.D. 570 in Mecca, now part of Saudi Arabia. His parents died when he was a child, and when he was older he became a camel driver and trader and had a wife and children. When Muhammad was about forty, the angel Gabriel visited him and shared with him the teachings of Allah (God). Such revelations were granted to Muhammad throughout the next twenty-two years. He compiled the messages in a book called the Qur'an (sometimes spelled Koran). The Qur'an is the holy book of Islam. Muslims believe it holds the exact words of Allah.

Illustration of Muhammad

When Muhammad began to share his message, he was not well received in Mecca. One of the tasks given to him by Allah was to rid the city of shrines to false gods. Many did not like this. Muhammad also taught the importance of equality and of charity toward the poor. It was wrong, he declared, to make money by charging high interest on loans to the poor. Moneylenders and other wealthy citizens didn't want to hear this.

Muhammad and his followers were forced to move to the nearby city of Yathrib, now named Medina. This journey became known as the *hijra,* or emigration. The hijra took place in A.D. 622, which became the year 1 on the Islamic calendar.

Muhammad gathered many followers in his new environment. Years later, when he returned to Mecca with huge crowds of believers, the people were ready to welcome him and follow his messages. Muhammad died a few months after his return to Mecca, but by then his teachings had taken hold.

The Islamic Calendar

The Islamic calendar is lunar, meaning that it is determined by the phases of the moon. A month is the period between two new moons. It differs from the calendar commonly used throughout the world, which is based on the solar year. Muslims follow both calendars, but the Islamic calendar determines their holy days. While the solar calendar has 365 days a year, the Islamic has 354 days. The beginning of the first month of the Islamic calendar year is Muharram, the Muslim New Year. This day commemorates the beginning of Islamic history, the day in 622 when Muhammad began the hijra from Mecca to Medina.

Soon Islam was spreading throughout the Middle East. Within 200 years, the faith had spread from Spain to India. In later centuries, Islam expanded as traders and missionaries carried the faith throughout the region. People of many ethnic backgrounds, speaking many languages, followed Islam. As they intermingled, Arabic became a common language throughout the region in business and writing. It helped to spread Islam farther.

The Teachings of Islam

Allah is the Arabic word for the same God that Christians and Jews worship. Many of the teachings in Islam, Christianity, and Judaism are similar. Muslims believe in guardian angels and in a final judgment, in which the good achieve complete happiness in heaven and the evil are sent to hell.

Islam is based on teachings from many prophets—people who Muslims believe were chosen by Allah to speak for him. Some Islamic prophets are mentioned in the Old Testament of the Bible, including Moses and Abraham. Muslims believe that Jesus was a great prophet too, but they don't believe as

The Five Pillars of Islam

Muslims follow five practices in an effort to live their faith. These are called the five pillars of Islam. The first is *Shahada*, the profession of faith. Muslims recite the words "There is no god but God, and Muhammad is the messenger of God." This belief is part of what separates Muslims from Christians and Jews.

The second pillar is *Salah*, the requirement to pray five times daily: at dawn, midday, midafternoon, sunset, and evening (left). The noon prayer on Fridays is usually said in a mosque. At other times, the prayers may be said anywhere—at home, school, or work. Muslims must purify themselves before prayer by washing their face, neck, hands, arms, and feet. Then they kneel and bow their head low to the ground as a way of showing their submission to Allah. While praying, they face the holy city of Mecca.

Muslims are required to give alms, or donations, to the poor. This is the third pillar, *Zakat*. Only people who are themselves very poor do not have to observe Zakat. Muslims are expected to give 2.5 percent of their income, but if they can afford to give more, it is considered a very good deed.

During the holy month of Ramadan, the ninth month of the Islamic calendar, Muslims observe the fourth pillar, *Saum*. During this time they are required to fast from dawn to dusk. Certain people, such as pregnant women, the elderly, and the very young, don't need to observe this rule. Others, however, may not eat or drink anything from sunup to sunset. Since the Islamic calendar is based on the moon, the dates of Ramadan shift each year. It is particularly difficult to fast

when Ramadan falls during summer months, when the day is longest. Such fasting takes great discipline, but Muslims believe it helps them focus on God rather than on the desires of their own bodies. It also helps them remember the poor who are often hungry. When the month ends, Muslims celebrate Eid al-Fitr, or the Festival of Breaking the Fast. This three-day celebration is one of Islam's most important holidays, and it is a joyous time for Muslims.

The final of the five pillars is *hajj*. This is the requirement that all Muslims try to make a pilgrimage, or visit, to Mecca at least once in their life (above). Pilgrims to Mecca wear white robes and pray at the Great Mosque there. While praying, they walk seven times around the Kaaba, the shrine that holds a black stone that Muslims believe was given to the prophet Abraham by God. It is Islam's most holy object. Other activities during the hajj include visiting the plain of Arafat, where Muhammad delivered his final sermon. Hajj should take place during the first or second week of the Muslim month of Zuul-Hijja. The pilgrimage symbolizes the unity and equality of all Muslims as they focus on God.

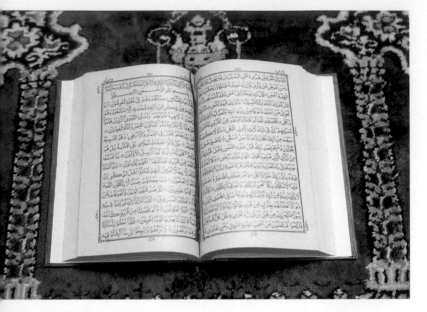

The Qur'an is Islam's
holy book.

Christians do that he was the Son of God. They believe that the revelations given by God to Muhammad are the most complete and accurate.

Muslims follow religious guidelines set down in the Qur'an. The Hadith is another Islamic source for truth and inspiration. It is a collection of sayings and decisions of Muhammad. When Muslims cannot find guidance for specific situations in either the Qur'an or the Hadith, they turn to Islamic judges. The judges rule base on similar circumstances found in the two books, or they consult with other wise Muslim leaders.

Sharia is the body of laws found in the Qur'an and the decisions of judges throughout Islamic history. Among other rules, Sharia prohibits Muslims from killing, stealing, lying, and drinking alcohol. They are instructed to dress and behave with modesty and to be charitable and fair. Muslims are not allowed to eat pork nor the meat of any animals that have died of natural causes. Muslim men may marry only Christian, Jewish, or Muslim women; Muslim women, however, may marry only Muslim men. This is because children are expected to follow the religion of their father: A Muslim man may marry someone of another faith because his children would still be considered Muslim.

Types of Islam

Following the death of Muhammad, the religion split into two groups with differing beliefs. The groups are called Sunnis and Shi'ites. The split began during a struggle for leadership following Muhammad's death. Each man seeking to be leader had his own group of followers. Shi'ites followed Muhammad's son-in-law, who was also his cousin. To this day, Shi'ites believe that a true leader of Islam must be a direct descendent of Muhammad. They believe that their imam, or spiritual guide, has God's authority to interpret the Qur'an. Sunnis, by contrast, believe that any leader who follows Sharia with fairness deserves Muslim support. The Qur'an itself is the final authority, according to Sunnis.

Sunnis make up the majority of the Muslim population in the Middle East. Large minorities of Shi'ites live in Kuwait, the United Arab Emirates, and the eastern province of Saudi Arabia. They are the majority in nearby Bahrain.

Muslims in Qatar

Qataris are nearly all members of a small faction of Sunni Muslims known as Wahhabis. Wahhabism is considered the official form of Islam in Qatar and Saudi Arabia. It follows the more traditional values and beliefs of early Islam. Its followers don't believe in saints, and they celebrate few religious holidays. They specifically avoid those that honor prophets, including Muhammad. Instead Wahhabis stress the unity and superiority of God, and they try to keep non-Muslim ideals from affecting their lives.

Muhammad ibn Abd al-Wahhab

Muhammad ibn Abd al-Wahhab, who lived in Saudi Arabia from 1703 to 1792, founded the Wahhabi Islam reform movement. Alarmed at the way some members of Bedouin tribes disrespected and ignored teachings from the Qur'an, he came to believe that every practice and belief added to Islam after the third century of the Muslim era, about A.D. 950, was not a true part of the faith. He returned Islam to what he believed to be a pure religion. In particular, he did not like the way some Muslims had begun praying to saints, making sacrificial offerings, living extravagantly, and making pilgrimages to special mosques.

Ibn Abd al-Wahhab instead wanted to return to focusing on God and the traditional practices of Islam. He believed in the importance of caring for the poor, praying at the obligatory times, and following the five pillars of Islam. He also believed that Muslims should dress simply, avoid smoking tobacco, and worship in plainly designed mosques.

Ibn Abd al-Wahhab felt that anyone who didn't share his beliefs were heretics, and thus he felt justified in using force to change the ways of such nonbelievers. He declared a holy war—a *jihad*—on neighboring tribes in Saudi Arabia, joining forces with a tribal chief named Muhammad Ibn Saud. The war continued for decades, even after ibn Abd al-Wahhab's death in 1792. Eventually, Wahhab's supporters were successful. By 1811, Wahhabism was the dominant form of Islam throughout all Arabia except Yemen. Since that time, Wahhabism has had periods of strength and weakness, but it remains the main form of Islam of Muslims in Qatar and Saudi Arabia.

Even though Wahhabism is a strict form of Islam, most Qataris take a fairly liberal approach to their faith. It is possible to purchase alcohol in Qatar, though most Muslims do not drink. Qatari women are allowed to drive cars. Since most Qataris are prosperous, they take seriously the third pillar of Islam, Zakat, which urges charity toward the poor. They support Muslim orphanages in poorer countries and Muslim widows whose husbands died in war.

Religious Holidays

Because Wahhabism is the official form of Islam in Qatar, Qataris do not celebrate all Muslim holidays. They do, however, mark the month of Ramadan with traditional fasting from sunrise to sunset. Muslims believe that by avoiding food, drinking, and smoking, they can more freely reflect on spiritual matters. Ramadan provides a time to build self-discipline, increase devotion to God, and grow in compassion for people who are less fortunate. Non-Muslims visiting in the country are expected to follow these restrictions too, at least while they are in public.

Each evening at sunset during Ramadan, families gather for their meal, called *iftar*. Night is a busy time for Qataris during this month, for they often gather to socialize and conduct business.

Eid al-Fitr, the three-day celebration marking Ramadan's end, is a joyful occasion in Qatar. Families celebrate with reunions and festive meals featuring delicious foods. They wear new clothing and buy gifts for their children. Fireworks light up the night sky.

Qataris also celebrate Eid al-Adha, or the Feast of Sacrifice, each year during the time of hajj. It is observed by those who travel to Mecca as well as by those who stay home, in remembrance of Abraham's willingness to sacrifice his son, Isma'il, to obey God. Qataris sacrifice a sheep, prepare the meat, and use some for a feast for themselves. They share the rest with friends and with the poor. During this three-day holiday, businesses are closed.

Religious Holidays in Qatar

Most Qataris are Wahhabi Muslims, who do not observe all the Muslim holidays. The religious holidays follow the Islamic calendar.

Ramadan	The ninth month of the Islamic year, marked by fasting from sunrise to sunset
Eid al-Fitr	A three-day celebration at the end of Ramadan
Eid al-Adha	A three-day holiday observed during the time of the annual pilgrimage to Mecca

Culture of Qatar

Q ATAR'S CULTURAL HISTORY IS A HISTORY OF THE LIVES, actions, and tales of the Bedouin people. Bedouins were desert nomads. Everything they owned they carried with them on their journeys. Each object had a purpose—they had no room to carry nonuseful things.

This nomadic life affected Bedouin culture and art. Even today, Qataris rarely create paintings or sculpture only for decoration, although their useful creations—rugs, blankets, and clothing—are beautifully embellished with color and embroidery. Qataris carefully weave baskets from palm leaves and cane in a process called *al-safaf*. They dye the hair of goats and

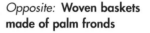

Opposite: **Woven baskets made of palm fronds**

Bedouins were known for their beautiful decoration of useful items, such as this embroidered cloth.

Gold jewelry at a gold souq

camels with vivid colors and weave it into saddlebags and bedding. Women's clothing for special occasions is stitched with gold thread.

Creating and wearing intricate gold jewelry is another Qatari tradition. Women wear the *al-tasa*, a lovely head ornament; the *al-kaff*, a large gold bracelet; and the *al-mirtaesha*, a full gold necklace that often covers the entire chest and waist area.

Bedouin people expressed their artistic ideas through music and dance. Traditional songs, performed by folksingers, dancers, and musicians, are common in Qatari celebrations and weddings. One of the traditional Bedouin dances, called the *ayyalah*, reenacts a battle. Two rows of dancers seem to fight each other. Performers move to drumbeats, swinging sticks and swords and singing challenges to one another. Copper cymbals and tambourines accompany them. Other instruments commonly used in Qatari music include the *oud* and the *rebaba*, both stringed instruments.

Two rows of people reenact a battle during this Raza warrior dance.

Qatari literary traditions are based on the spoken word. Bedouins shared poetry and folktales and passed them down from generation to generation. They did not have a strong history of printed books for, again, that would mean carrying things along with them. But life is different in Qatar today. The printed word is gaining popularity. Abdel Rahman al-Mannai has written a play titled *Umm Zinn*, "The Most Beautiful," in the Qatari dialect of Arabic. He has also made American and British plays available to Qataris by translating them into Arabic.

Museums

Exhibits in the country's museums represent much of Qatar's rich culture. The Ethnographic Museum, a few blocks from the corniche in Doha, is in a home built about a hundred years ago and restored to its original beauty. Visitors see a glimpse of life in old Doha, before the oil boom transformed the city.

The Doha Fort is even older than the Ethnographic Museum. It was built in the nineteenth century by the Ottoman Turks. They were allowed to keep a garrison (military post) in

The Doha Fort is now a popular museum.

The Weaponry Museum displays items used in wars throughout Qatar's history.

Doha, thanks to a treaty signed with Shaykh Jassim bin Muhammad. The fort houses several displays of various aspects of life in Doha as it was more than a century ago. They include rope making, shipbuilding, goldsmithing, weaving, stone carving, and fishing.

Other Doha museums include the Weaponry Museum, which houses a large collection of swords, guns, daggers, and other weapons used in regional wars throughout Qatari history. The Postal Museum draws many stamp collectors and others interested in the country's postal history.

The Qatar National Museum and Aquarium

The palace of Shaykh Abdalla bin Jassim al-Thani, emir from 1913 to 1949, is now the Qatar National Museum. This grand building on Doha's corniche was restored in the 1980s and is part of a complex that includes a marine museum and an aquarium. It's Qatar's largest museum.

Qatar's geology is the topic of one of the museum's main displays. Its shows how the land that is now Qatar was formed. It also highlights the plant and animal life of the country. There is an interesting archaeological display that includes pots and arrowheads from the country's early history. Another display shows how sailors from ancient times used the sun and stars to help them navigate the seas. A courtyard within the museum is surrounded by rooms that are filled with items illustrating traditional lifestyles in Qatar. They offer glimpses of how ancient people lived and furnished their rooms. The courtyard itself holds three homes that were once inhabited by the shaykh's family.

The Marine Museum located next to the main National Museum building instructs visitors about the history of sailing on the Qatar coast, the pearl industry, fishing, and boat building. The aquarium in the basement level of the Marine Museum houses turtles and other marine life. Information is printed in Arabic and in English, to accommodate the many international visitors to the country.

Sports in Qatar

Soccer is a popular sport in Qatar, just as it is in many other countries throughout the world. Doha alone has fourteen soccer stadiums, and others dot the country. One of the most exciting events in Qatari soccer history was when the national soccer team reached the quarterfinals at the summer Olympics in Barcelona, Spain, in 1996.

Qatar played Jordan (in red) in the 1998 Arab Cup.

Most Qataris live in coastal towns, and for sports, many head to the calm waters of the Persian Gulf. Sailing dhows—traditional wooden sailing boats—is a popular sport. Several international sailing races take place off the coast of Qatar. Doha has a sailing school and three sailing clubs, and it hosts regular regattas during a season that runs from September through June.

The beaches between Doha and Messaieed are some of the country's best, and swimming is another popular activity in Qatar. Water-skiing and wind surfing are popular here. Swimmers must remember, though, to respect the local religious

Dhows are traditional sailing boats.

values and wear modest swimming suits. Wearing bikinis or other revealing suits is considered disrespectful.

Some people snorkel and scuba dive off the coast of Qatar to see coral and crustaceans. But the water is so salty that few fish live there, and jellyfish, sea snakes, and poisonous dragonfish swim nearby. What's more, strong currents can pull a swimmer off course.

Doha is preparing to host the Asian Games of 2006. It is a prestigious major multisport competition similar to the summer Olympics, and Qatar worked hard to bring the games to its capital. It's now working even harder to get ready for the event, spending U.S. $1 billion to construct the necessary stadiums and sports fields as well as an athletes' village. The games are expected to draw thousands of visitors to the country.

Marriage Customs in Qatar

Marriages in Qatar are typically arranged by the couples' elders—fathers, brothers, and uncles—and reflect the unions that will have the best effect on the families' social status and on any business partnerships between families. Most Qataris marry within their tribe—that is, they marry someone in their large extended family. Qataris wishing to marry people of other nationalities must obtain permission from the Ministry of the Interior, and permission is not always granted.

In Qatar girls sometimes marry as young as fourteen or fifteen. Until recently it was common for girls to marry at twelve, but today families wait until girls have completed their education. Boys marry when they are a bit older. The groom's family pays a bridal dowry of money called a *mahr* to the bride's family before the wedding. Then the elaborate ceremonies begin, with

separate ceremonies for the men and the women. The rituals and celebrations often last for days.

Al-Jazeera

Al-Jazeera, the first independent Arabic-language television channel, founded in 1996, is based in Qatar. It broadcasts exclusively news and information programming. It receives financial support from the Qatari government but has been allowed to broadcast without government control. *Al-Jazeera* means "peninsula," referring to Qatar's location. When it began, it ran only six hours of programming a day. Now it operates round the clock. Satellites transmit programs to more than 35 million viewers throughout the Middle East, Africa, North America, and Europe. It employs more than 600 journalists.

Al-Jazeera is unusual in the Middle East in that it is commercially oriented and not run by a government agency. It honors Islam's traditions and customs, but it also freely criticizes government policies and actions. One of its most popular shows, *The Opposite Direction*, pairs speakers with differing viewpoints to discuss cultural and political topics. Viewers are encouraged to call in to voice their opinions. Such freedom of expression is unusual in the Arab media, and it has proven very controversial. Many leaders of other countries in the Arab world have complained, and some have even discontinued their diplomatic relations with Qatar. But Al-Jazeera thrives on the controversy and continues to draw viewers. For the Qatari government, it offers a means of creating a distinct identity for Qatar. The emir is working to bring democracy to Qatar, and this freedom of the press is a part of that.

Al-Jazeera with head-quarters in Doha draws viewers around the world.

Al-Jazeera's worldwide audience has grown enormously since September 11, 2001, when terrorists attacked the World Trade Center in New York and the Pentagon in Washington, D.C. The station received and broadcast video messages from Osama bin Laden. The English-language version of its broadcast, launched in 2003, increased its viewership even more.

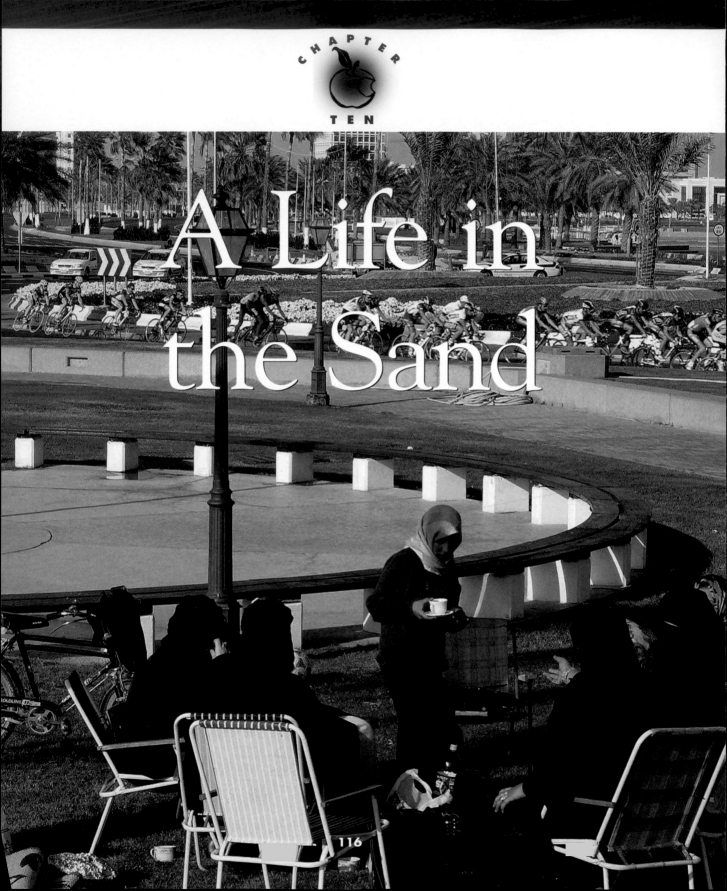

A Life in the Sand

MEALS IN QATAR TRADITIONALLY HAVE BEEN MADE UP of the common foods of the Arab world. These foods have their roots in the Bedouin lifestyle, in which people could easily pack up and move from place to place. Such foods included rice, dates, and dried meats.

Today, as the country has become more modern and people have settled into urban areas, Qatari cuisine has opened to other influences. Days begin early in Qatar, so *al-futuur*, breakfast, is usually eaten at about 6 A.M. It is a light meal and usually consists of something that can be prepared and served easily. Common breakfast foods include cheeses, yogurt, fresh fruit, and coffee.

Qataris' main meal is *al-ghada*, lunch, which they eat at around 1 P.M. Family members come home from work and school to eat together. They often have appetizers followed by a stew served with bread, fruits, and vegetables. They take time to rest after the meal before they return to work. Dinner, *al-asha'*, is typically a light meal featuring sandwiches and other simple foods. It is usually served late in the evening.

Qatar's geography also influences its food choices. Seafood is a popular mealtime choice. Qataris enjoy crab, lobster, tuna, snapper, kingfish, and shrimp. Another favorite meat is lamb, but most Qataris do not eat pork because Islam prohibits it. Some traditional Qatari foods include *hareis*, which is lamb and wheat cooked slowly together; and *matchbous*, also lamb and rice, to which special spices are added. *Umm Ali* is a bread-pudding

Fafafa

One of Qatar's most popular native foods is also one of its most expensive, because it is so rare. *Fafafa* is a fungus that grows wild in the desert. If it's not cooked correctly it can make people very sick, but prepared properly it is delicious. Many Qataris enjoy traveling into the desert to seek out this treat.

dessert; other favorite sweets include a cheesecake called *al-shasaraya* and *mehalabiya*, a type of pistachio pudding.

Some Qatari food favorites are typical throughout the Arab world. Hummus, a dip made of crushed chickpeas seasoned with sesame seeds, is one. Others include *tabbouleh*, a salad made with crushed wheat, mint, diced tomatoes, onion, and parsley; *waraq ainab*, grape leaves stuffed with ground meat and rice; and *koussa mahshi*, stuffed zucchini.

Hummus is a popular Qatari food.

Foreigners working and living in Qatar have brought their own flavors. Among the foreign-influenced foods in Qatar are curry-flavored dishes from Pakistan and India. These are eaten using flat bread instead of silverware to scoop the food. American influences have brought to Qatar a love of fast-food such as hamburgers and fries. Restaurants such as Pizza Hut, Kentucky Fried Chicken, and McDonald's do a good business in Qatar.

Most Arabs love freshly ground coffee, *qahwa*, and prepare it very strong. It is traditionally served to guests with fresh dates. The dates are very sweet and are delicious

between sips of the hot qahwa. Other common beverages are tea and cardamom-flavored coffee. A guest who is offered such a refreshment would be considered rude if he or she refused. The giving and receiving of food and drink are important in Qatari culture.

Alcohol is forbidden by Muslim tradition, so beverages such as beer and wine are rarely available in Qatar. It is possible to order alcohol in a few of the nightclubs in the major international hotels in Doha, where foreigners tend to stay.

Coffee is a favorite beverage for most Qataris.

Male traditional dress is the dishdasha.

Clothing

Men in Qatar usually wear a long, white cotton robe known as the *dishdasha*. This traditional garb is usually worn with a *ghutrah*, or headcloth, also of white cotton. An *uqal*, a twisted piece of black cloth, holds the ghutrah in place. For special occasions, men may also wear a *bisht*— a dark, beautiful coat embellished with intricate embroidery.

The *abaya*, a long black gown, is the traditional clothing of Qatari women in public. The law does not require this, but a great majority of women still choose to wear it anyway. Some say their decision to

Female traditional dress is the abaya.

Made to Fit

When most people in North America want new clothes, they go to a store and purchase something that has already been made. It's different in Qatar. There, people visit skilled crafts-people, select fabrics and styles, and order clothing specially made for them. Dressmakers usually need only a day to complete a dress; tailors need a few days to make a suit. Buyers have a huge choice of fabrics, and they don't pay much for the labor, so most people are satisfied with this method of purchasing new clothing.

wear the abaya reflects their right to choose and that the abaya gives women the freedom to move about as they want and wear what they wish underneath it, without worrying about drawing attention to their bodies.

Underneath the abaya, Qatari women typically wear long gowns. A few women, particularly those who are moving into the political and business world, now wear Western-style skirts and jackets or dresses. Those who choose not to wear the abaya will often wear a veil over their hair.

Most new homes under construction in Doha are large.

The Home

Qatar is a wealthy nation, and the homes of its citizens reflect this. Most are quite large, usually with one large living room on the main floor and a few smaller living rooms, as well as a majlis, a sitting room reserved only for men. Bedrooms and bathrooms are usually above the ground floor. The architecture is traditionally ornate and includes decorative wooden panels, porches and balconies, and arched windows.

Incense

Most Qataris enjoy using incense to add a pleasing fragrance in their homes, a common practice throughout most of the Persian Gulf region. *Mijmars*, incense burners, are used frequently by nearly every family. Most mijmars are made of clay, with a bowl at the bottom for a few hot coals. The coals are then covered with any of several types of incense. One is frankincense, a dried resin that originates in Yemen or Oman.

Another is sandalwood, a fragrant wood that is quite expensive. Some people create their own mixtures of woods and resins that can be purchased at local souqs. All fill the home with a pleasant-smelling smoke. When company is present, the mijmar is often brought out toward the end of the visit and passed around to guests, so that when they leave, their clothes will carry the scent of the incense.

Education

Qatar's education system has grown rapidly since the discovery of oil in the country. Before then, only some of Qatar's boys were educated through the primary grades at a handful of schools. The country's first school opened in 1952.

Today the government has a large education budget and guarantees free education. Boys and girls attend school separately.

Qatari children must attend six years of primary school, three years of middle school, and three years of secondary schooling. They usually begin classes by 7 A.M. and finish at 1 P.M. Students in secondary school are able to concentrate on a certain area of study. They can specialize in business training, technical education, religious studies, or teacher training.

Though children of foreign workers living in Qatar are eligible for free public schooling, many choose private schools so that the children are schooled in their own culture and native

Girls and boys attend seperate classes.

A Qatari man prepares for a good career during a university chemistry class.

language. This is especially true for children of workers from India.

Qatari students can attend the large University of Qatar in Doha after completing secondary school. The university opened in 1977 and has about nine thousand students today. The campus is divided into two sections, one for men and one for women. Departments focus on engineering, humanities, Islam, science, social studies, and teacher training. The Qatari government also provides scholarships for about one thousand students each year to attend universities in the United States, Europe, and other Arab countries.

Health Care

Just as the discovery of oil helped to finance improvements in Qatar's education system, it has also brought about positive changes in health care. Disease and early death were once common in Qatar. Today Qatar offers its citizens some of the best health care in the world.

Qataris receive free medical and dental treatment, as well as free major hospital procedures and stays. Foreigners living in the country can get treatment in the same facilities; however, they must pay for much of their care. The Ministry of Health runs the country's medical system. Many of the

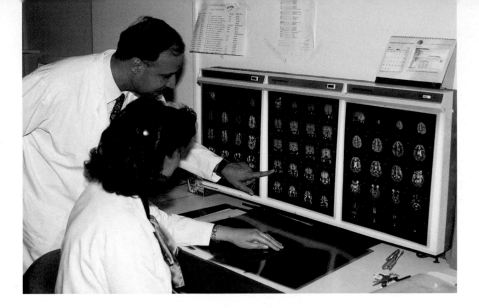

Hamad Medical Corporation Hospital in Doha provides quality health care to Qataris.

nation's doctors and nurses are foreigners, although more Qataris are filling those positions.

Leisure

Qataris enjoy a variety of activities during their free time. A favorite family outing in Doha is a trip to Aladdin's Kingdom. This amusement park is based on the traditional Arabic story of Aladdin and a genie who lived in an oil lantern. The park has grown each year since it opened in 1994; today it features many rides and activities, including a Magic Bus, a Ferris wheel, bumper boats, a carousel, and a train that circles the park. More-adventurous thrill-seekers enjoy the Thunder Bullet roller coaster, race-car

An amusement park during the International Winter Festival in January 2003

Children's Games

Children enjoy playing several traditional games in Qatar. Some of these are games that their parents and grandparents played when they were young. In one game, called *al-Ghomaid*, one boy is blindfolded and has to try to catch another of the boys, who are running around and making noise to try to confuse him.

The first person the blindfolded boy catches then wears the blindfold, and they start over.

In a girls' game, called *Umm al-lal*, one girl plays a wolf. She chases another girl who pretends to be a mother protecting her children from the wolf. Other girls portray the children.

rides, and the Aerotrim—a ride that simulates the flight of fighter pilots and astronauts. The park also features video games, costumed characters, and daily parades.

Camping is another activity some Qatari families enjoy. Though there are few designated campgrounds in Qatar, some people like to travel to the desert and live in tents for several days. This gives them the opportunity to experience the challenge of nature and enjoy its beauty.

Many families enjoy a walk along the corniche in Doha. The path is curving, clean, and colorful, filled with flowers, shrubs, and palm trees. It's a popular place to jog, stroll, and meet friends. People can also charter rides around the bay in Doha on traditional wooden sailboats called dhows.

Those looking for an activity that's a little more thrilling might head to the southeast part of Qatar for an exciting

Sand Skiing

Imagine swishing down the slopes on skies in the midst of a desert. It's not a joke! Sand skiing is growing in popularity in the deserts of Qatar. The silky sands of the high dunes around Messaieed make a great base for a swift run downhill. Another sport catching on is sand-surfing on a special surfboard.

desert drive. Qatar has some of the most beautiful sand dunes in the Persian Gulf region, and traveling in a four-wheel-drive vehicle is really the only way to see them up close. A popular spot to cruise is around the Khor al-Udeid, the Inland Sea. Here the sun and shadows play against golden sand, while the water and the sky shine a vivid blue. Dunes rise up high and cover vast areas. The scene is breathtaking.

Qatar is a lively, friendly nation, with plenty to do and see. The economy is healthy, and it is a democracy on the move. Qatar and its citizens have a great future in store.

Doha's walk along the corniche is refreshing.

Tourists enjoy four-wheel driving at Khor al-Udeid.

Timeline

Qatar History

People move into Qatar peninsula.	**c. 48000** B.C.
Hunters and fishers live along Qatar's coast.	**c. 5000** B.C.
Islam spreads throughout Qatar.	**c. A.D. 630**

World History

2500 B.C.	Egyptians build the Pyramids and the Sphinx in Giza.
563 B.C.	The Buddha is born in India.
A.D. 313	The Roman emperor Constantine recognizes Christianity.
610	The prophet Muhammad begins preaching a new religion called Islam.
1054	The Eastern (Orthodox) and Western (Roman) Churches break apart.
1066	William the Conqueror defeats the English in the Battle of Hastings.
1095	Pope Urban II proclaims the First Crusade.
1215	King John seals the Magna Carta.
1300s	The Renaissance begins in Italy.
1347	The Black Death sweeps through Europe.
1453	Ottoman Turks capture Constantinople, conquering the Byzantine Empire.
1492	Columbus arrives in North America.
1500s	The Reformation leads to the birth of Protestantism.
1776	The Declaration of Independence is signed.
1789	The French Revolution begins.

Qatar History (continued)

Britain and Portugal fight for control of Persian Gulf.	**c. 1600**
Sailors and traders from Kuwait settle on Qatar's northwest coast.	**1766**
Britain takes control of Persian Gulf.	**1800s**
Rahmah bin Jabir becomes first in a series of leaders in the Qatari peninsula. Wahhabis establish strong hold in Qatar.	**Early 1800s**
Rahmah bin Jabir is ousted from Qatar.	**1816**
General Treaty of Peace signed by British East India Company and area shaykhs.	**1820**

Qatar History

Doha bombed by British East India Company vessel.	1821
Warriors from Bahrain loot Doha and al-Wakrah. Peace treaty signed, in which Britain offers protection to Qatar; Shaykh Muhammad bin al-Thani becomes first emir of Qatar.	1868
Shaykh Jassim bin Muhammad al-Thani becomes emir of Qatar.	1878
Ottomans invade Qatar, establish base in Doha.	1893
Shaykh Abdalla bin Jassim al-Thani becomes emir of Qatar.	1913
Ottomans forced out of Doha.	1915
Oil exploration begins in Qatar.	1935
Oil discovered in Qatar.	1939
Shaykh Ali bin Abdalla al-Thani becomes emir of Qatar; oil is first exported from Qatar.	1949
Shaykh Hamad bin Ali al-Thani becomes emir of Qatar.	1960
Qatar declares independence.	1971
Shaykh Khalifa bin Hamad al-Thani becomes emir of Qatar after forcing out his cousin.	1972
Qatar joins Gulf War on side of United States.	1990
Diplomatic and economic relations established with Israel.	1993
Sheikh Hamad bin Khalifa al-Thani becomes emir after forcing his father out of office.	1995
First elections held in Qatar; women are allowed to vote and run for office.	1999

World History

1865	The American Civil War ends.
1914	World War I breaks out.
1917	The Bolshevik Revolution brings communism to Russia.
1929	Worldwide economic depression begins.
1939	World War II begins, following the German invasion of Poland.
1945	World War II ends.
1957	The Vietnam War starts.
1969	Humans land on the moon.
1975	The Vietnam War ends.
1979	Soviet Union invades Afghanistan.
1983	Drought and famine in Africa.
1989	The Berlin Wall is torn down as communism crumbles in Eastern Europe.
1991	Soviet Union breaks into separate states.
1992	Bill Clinton is elected U.S. president.
2000	George W. Bush is elected U.S. president.
2001	Terrorists attack World Trade Towers, New York, and the Pentagon, Washington, D.C.

Fast Facts

Official name: Dawlat Qatar (State of Qatar)

Capital: Doha

Official language: Arabic

Doha

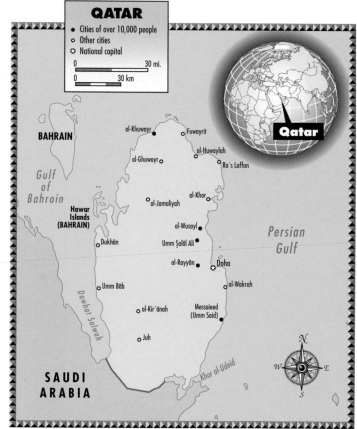

Qatar's flag

The Arabian Oryx is Qatar's national animal.

Official religion: Islam

Year of founding: 1971

National anthem: "Al-Salam al-Amiri" ("The Amiri Anthem")

Government: Constitutional emirate

Head of state: Emir

Head of government: Prime minister

Area of country: 4,416 square miles (11,437 sq km)

Greatest distance north to south: 115 miles (185 km)

Greatest distance east to west: 55 miles (89 km)

Land and water borders: Qatar's only land boundary is with Saudi Arabia. It is surrounded on the west, north, and east by the Persian Gulf.

Highest elevation: Qurayn Abu al-Bawl, 338 feet (103 m)

Lowest elevation: Sea level, at the coast

Highest average temperature: 104°F (40°C) in the summer

Lowest average temperature: 68°F (20°C) in the winter

Average annual precipitation: Less than 2 inches (5 cm)

The corniche

Currency

National population:	793,341	
Population of largest cities:	Doha	318,500
	al-Rayyān	194,800
	al-Wakrah	24,400
	Umm Salal	19,200
	Messaieed	9,000

Famous landmarks:
▶ *Khor al-Udeid,* the Inland Sea, at the southeast tip of Qatar

▶ *The National Museum*, Doha

▶ *The corniche*, Doha

▶ *Qurayn Abu al-Bawl*, the nation's highest point, in Jebel Dukhan

▶ *North Field*, a large natural-gas field just off the northern tip of Qatar

Industry: Crude oil and natural gas are the major products exported from Qatar. Sulfur and limestone are mined heavily as well. The most common manufactured products are cement, steel, and the fertilizer urea.

Currency: Qatar's currency is the Qatari riyal. One riyal is worth 100 dirhams. One U.S. dollar is equal to 3.64 riyals. This is a fixed rate.

System of weights and measures: metric system

Qatari children

Common Qatari words and phrases:

as-saláamu :alái-kum	Hello (literally, "Peace be with you")
wa :alái-kum as-saláam	Reply to "hello"
al-Hámdu li-l-láah	Praise be to God
Sabáah al-kháir	Good morning
Sabáah an-núur	Reply to "good morning"
Masáa' al-kháir	Good evening
Masáa an-núur	Reply to "good evening"
Shukran	Thank you
Má:a l-ásaf	I am sorry

Famous Qataris:

Rahmah bin Jabir
Qatari shaykh and pirate

Shaykh Muhammad bin al-Thani
First emir of Qatar

Abdel Rahman al-Mannai
Qatari playwright

Shaykh Hamad bin Khalifa al-Thani
Current emir of Qatar

Shayka Mouza bint Nasser al-Misnad
First lady of Qatar

Shayka Mouza bint Nasser al-Misnad

To Find Out More

Nonfiction

▶ Ali, Maureen. *The Middle East*. Englewood Cliffs, New Jersey: Silver Burdett Press, 1988.

▶ Mason, Antony. *Middle East*. Englewood Cliffs, New Jersey: Silver Burdett Press, 1988.

▶ Morrison, Ian. *Middle East*. Austin, Texas: Steck-Vaughn Library, 1991.

▶ Smart, Jack and Frances Altorfer. *Gulf Arabic*. Lincolnwood, Illinois: NTC/Contemporary Publishing, 1999.

Web Sites

▶ **The World Factbook**
www.cia.gov/cia/publications/factbook/geos/qa.html
Statistics about Qatar's demographics, geography, economy, and government.

▶ **Qatar Info**
www.qatar-info.com
General information on Qatari lifestyles and history.

▶ Qatar—A Cultural Profile Project
www.settlement.org/cp/english/qatar/
index.html
*Useful information about Qatar's
culture and society.*

▶ Ministry of Foreign Affairs
english.mofa.gov.qa/
*Official Qatari Web site, with
information on the country's
government, economy, history,
and tourism.*

Organizations

▶ Embassy of the State of Qatar
4200 Wisconsin Avenue NW
Washington, DC 20016
(202) 237-0061

Index

Page numbers in *italics* indicate illustrations.

Meet the Author

W HENEVER TERRI WILLIS BEGINS RESEARCHING A TOPIC for a book, she feels as though she is at the start of a journey.

"I spend so much time reading and thinking about the countries as I write about them, I sometimes feel like I'm there," she says.

The journey begins at the local library, where Terri checks out all the materials she can find on a country—books, magazines, and videos. She spends several days poring over all the information, to get a feel for where she'll be going with the book.

Bookstores often provide more materials. Good travel guides can be very helpful. They often contain a lot of great information about the nation and its people, as well as beautiful photography.

Then Terri heads to Memorial Library at the University of Wisconsin-Madison. "It's always fun to go back to the campus where I earned my degree," she says. "The library there is full of treasures."

Much of the material from university libraries is very technical and detailed. It takes time to go through the information carefully and present it in a way that young people understand.

The Internet is another good source for material. It's important to use only reliable sources, though, Terri warns. Anybody can create a Web site and put anything on it that he or she wants, so not all Internet content is credible. Terri is careful to use only information that comes from such places as universities and government agencies. Even then, she says, it's good to remember that some of these sources may not present the whole picture. A thorough search is important.

Terri fills out her research by talking to people and asking questions. Embassies, chambers of commerce, government agencies, universities—all have knowledgeable people who are willing to help.

Terri has a degree in journalism. Her books include *Libya*, *Romania*, *Vietnam*, and *Venezuela* in the Enchantment of the World series. Other books she has written for Children's Press include *Land Use and Abuse*, *Cars: an Environmental Challenge* (co-authored by Wallace B. Black), and *Restoring Nature, Land*.

Terri lives in Cedarburg, Wisconsin, with her husband, Harry, and their two daughters, Andrea and Elizabeth.

Photo Credits

Photographs © 2004:

AKG-Images, London: 44 right
AP/Wide World Photos: 60 left
(Richard Drew), 38, 125 bottom
(Wally Santana), 12
Byron Augustin: 42, 82, 91, 106
(Rebecca Augustin), 15, 16, 20, 21,
22 top, 22 bottom, 27, 29, 43, 47 top,
53, 58, 62, 72, 73, 74 right, 78, 79,
80, 90, 93, 104, 109, 112, 119, 121,
122, 123, 124, 125 top, 127 bottom,
133 top
Corbis Images: 10, 96 (Bettmann),
32 bottom (Pam Gardner), 81
(Robert Holmes), 51 (Hulton/
Deutsch Collection), 48 (Khaled
Mouftah/AFP Photo), 7 top, 68,
130 left (Christine Osborne), 67
(Reuters News Media, Inc.), 30
(Scott T. Smith), 18, 107 (Arthur
Thevenart), 75
Corbis Sygma: 2 (Jacques Langevin),
120 top (Attar Maher)
Getty Images: 61, 63 bottom, 65 (AFP),
9, 84, 98 (Carlo Allegri), 115
(Joseph Barrak/AFP), 92 (Patrick
Baz/AFP), 60 right (Ho/QNA/AFP),
83 bottom, 83 top, 88, 132 bottom
(Karim Jaafar/AFP), 13, 63 top
(Nicholas Kamm/AFP), 120 bottom
(Robert Sullivan/AFP)

Hulton | Archive/Getty Images: 55
Landov, LLC/Reuters: 57, 133 bottom
(Ray Stubblebine), 113 (Yu Sung-Ho)
Mary Evans Picture Library: 46 bottom,
46 top
Minden Pictures: 32 top (Michael &
Patricia Fogden), 31 (Frans Lanting),
35 (Norbert Wu)
Peter Arnold Inc.: 33 (Fred Bruemmer),
39 (M. Gunther/Bios)
Photo Researchers, NY: 17 (Geospace/
SPL), 34, 131 bottom (Tom McHugh)
PictureQuest/BananaStock Ltd.: 118
Reuters: 7 bottom, 37 (Chris Helgren),
111 (Fatih Saribas)
Sipa Press: 70, 116
The Art Archive/Picture Desk: 45
(Dagli Orti/Biblioteca Estense
Modena)
The Image Works: 114 (Hinata
Haga/HAGA), 99 (Kazuyoshi
Nomachi/HAGA)
TRIP Photo Library: 36 (B. Gadsby),
cover, 6, 8, 26, 28, 41, 69 top, 71,
87, 94, 100, 105, 108, 110, 127 top,
132 top.

Maps by XNR Productions Inc.